My Journey with the Lord

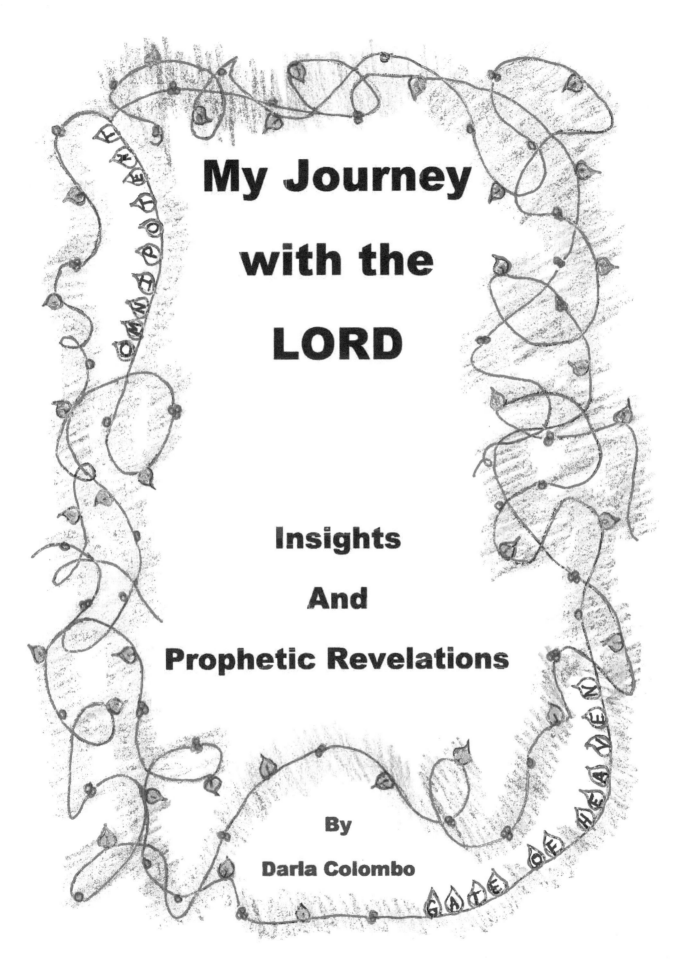

My Journey with the LORD

Insights

And

Prophetic Revelations

By

Darla Colombo

XULON PRESS

Xulon Press
2301 Lucien Way #415
Maitland, FL 32751
407.339.4217
www.xulonpress.com

Printed in the United States of America.

ISBN-13: 9781545624241

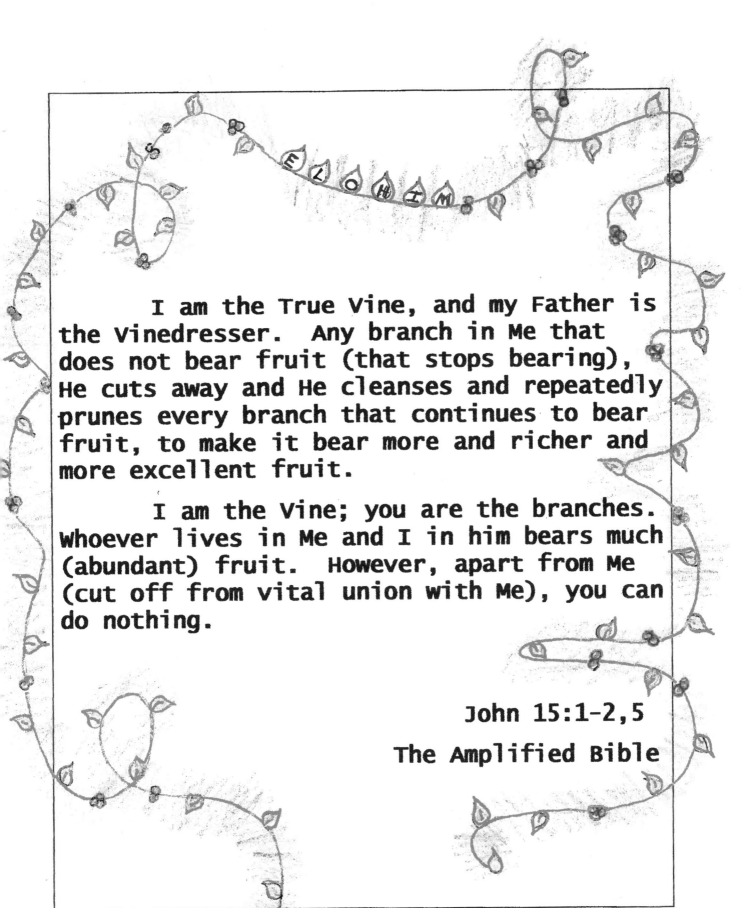

I am the True Vine, and my Father is the Vinedresser. Any branch in Me that does not bear fruit (that stops bearing), He cuts away and He cleanses and repeatedly prunes every branch that continues to bear fruit, to make it bear more and richer and more excellent fruit.

I am the Vine; you are the branches. Whoever lives in Me and I in him bears much (abundant) fruit. However, apart from Me (cut off from vital union with Me), you can do nothing.

John 15:1-2,5

The Amplified Bible

AUTHOR'S NOTE

Following is a copy of a journal entry that was written almost two years ago. God reveals His purpose and plan for each of us when we are open to His voice. Sometimes we don't even realize truth until we look back on our life and SEE what the Lord has declared.

2-15-16

Father I was reading in <u>The Courts of Heaven</u> that in "Eph. 2:10 the word *workmanship* in Greek means a poem. We are God's poem that was written in Heaven before we were born. We are a poem with a point." God created us to be His message – I, Darla Colombo, was a poem written before I was born. This poem contains good works that were written before I ever came to be in this earthly realm. I was a scroll written in Heaven with poetic power that now has been birth into this earthly arena. The writings of Heaven became flesh on Earth when I was born. Father, Daddy, that same writing flows out of me in poetic form as messages from Heaven coming forth into this Earthly atmosphere. Your Heavenly Words speak forth life, health, wholeness, revelation, and judgment into the atmosphere surrounding Your children. Let Your hand be upon my hand, guiding and directing each thought, each word that announces Your plans and purposes that will be accomplished in this Earthly Realm. So be it (Amen).

What was once a poem [words written within the Word (Jesus Christ)] has now been birthed into the earthly realm. That Heavenly poem (me) will birth the good works that the Lord called forth – as long as I stay connected to that Heavenly Word.

Lord, let the works and the words that were written in that Heavenly poem come forth through poetic poems and poetic messages here in this Earthly atmosphere with power! Let my thoughts, my words, and my writings be filled with Heaven's language, Heaven's creativity, and Heaven's anointing to save, to anoint, to saturate, to guide, to fill, to set free, to uplift, and to consume all Your love.

I'm amazed by the anointing of the Holy Spirit, who prepares us for good works that have been deposited into our hearts for a future time. Even when we do not grasp God's plan, His purpose WILL come to pass.

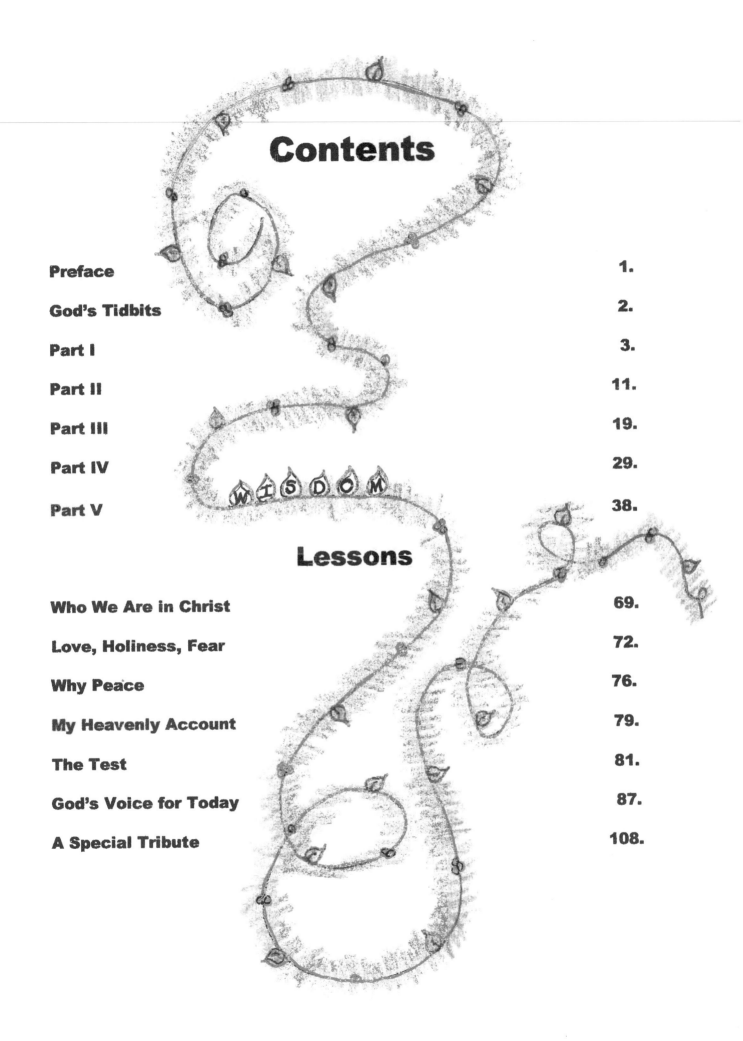

Contents

Lessons

LOVE

As we travel the roadway of life, we are never alone. A loving, tender Father guides, directs, and orders our path. Whether we travel across the meadows, through the valley, or over the mountain, God is faithful. When the battle is intense, He shields us with His armor; when the storms rage, He plants our feet; when the waters swell, He lifts us on His wings. God is watchful of His Word!

I want to thank my Heavenly Father, 'Daddy', for the poems, *maskil, that He has placed in my spirit to shepherd, sustain, and strengthen me when my world seemed to tumble down. Each word and each thought lifted me higher and surrounded my heart with a peace that no person could understand. It is my prayer that each gift God has placed in my spirit will bring healing and wisdom to the ones who journey with me through the pages of this book. God's Word and His message announce truth and generate light to the eyes, knowledge to the mind, and joy to the soul.

My parents, Mr. and Mrs. Robert Linville; my children (Andrew, Robert, and Alison) and their families; and my church family have loved me when I've been unlovable, forgiven me when I've fallen, and encouraged me when I've failed. Thank you for the privilege and honor of knowing you and being a part of your lives.

As you read the last part of this book; you will notice a change in the way the Lord speaks. His Words are more prophetic about the times and seasons of our day. I believe the Holy Spirit is speaking to His people and calling them higher. His voice announces truth, and we need to heed His warnings.

*maskil/mas kil/ Hebrew word meaning instructional poem

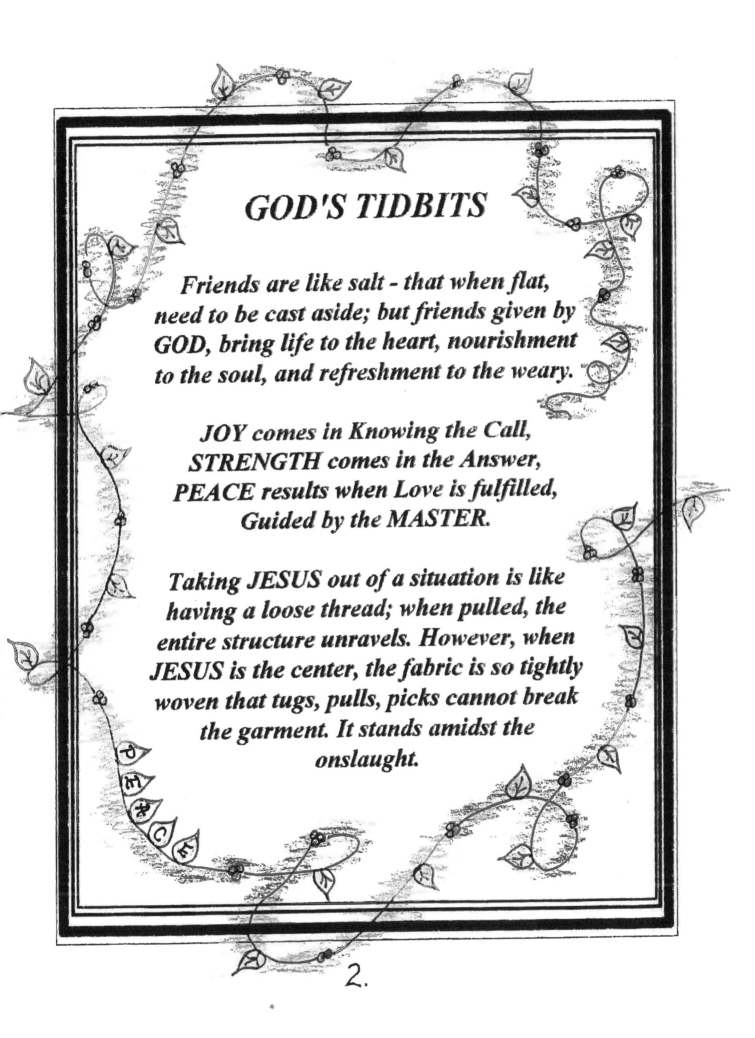

GOD'S TIDBITS

Friends are like salt - that when flat, need to be cast aside; but friends given by GOD, bring life to the heart, nourishment to the soul, and refreshment to the weary.

JOY comes in Knowing the Call, STRENGTH comes in the Answer, PEACE results when Love is fulfilled, Guided by the MASTER.

Taking JESUS out of a situation is like having a loose thread; when pulled, the entire structure unravels. However, when JESUS is the center, the fabric is so tightly woven that tugs, pulls, picks cannot break the garment. It stands amidst the onslaught.

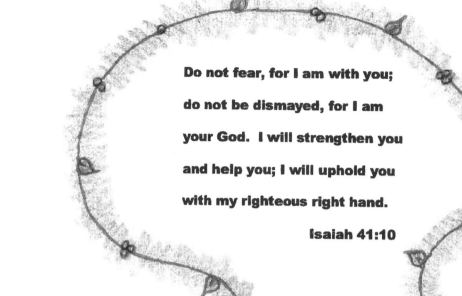

Do not fear, for I am with you;

do not be dismayed, for I am

your God. I will strengthen you

and help you; I will uphold you

with my righteous right hand.

Isaiah 41:10

As I began my walk with the LORD, I discovered that each day was like a new rose bud on a vine. Sometimes the rose bud opens pedal by pedal, absorbing each drop of dew that falls to the ground. Often though, in order to survive, the rose has to fight against drought, predators, or man-made enemies. With each battle the rose grows stronger and stronger until finally it stands triumphant amid GOD's creation. So is our walk with our SAVIOR. Every aspect of our life is a bridge from one path to another. When the weariness of the struggle overwhelms us, GOD's hand supports us and takes us to a new level where spring rains refresh our weary souls.

Part 1 of this book is dedicated to the battles and skirmishes my 'DADDY' has led me through and to the valuable lessons learned. As you read each poem, my prayer is that you will be lifted above the storm and carried to a loving FATHER's arms.

PART I

Battles and Lessons

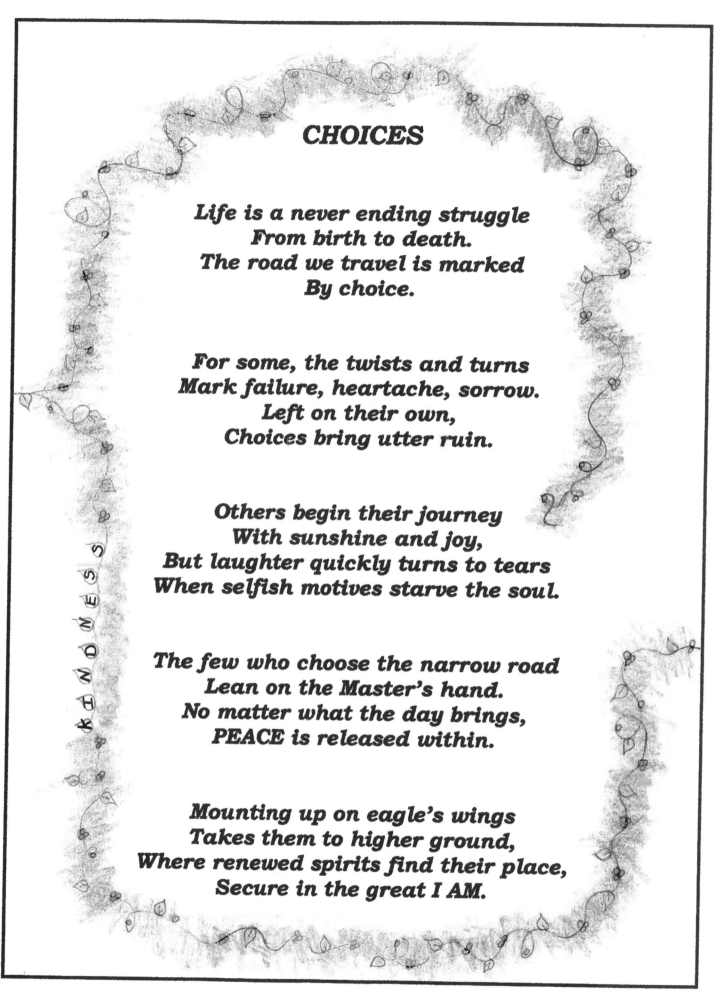

CHOICES

Life is a never ending struggle
From birth to death.
The road we travel is marked
By choice.

For some, the twists and turns
Mark failure, heartache, sorrow.
Left on their own,
Choices bring utter ruin.

Others begin their journey
With sunshine and joy,
But laughter quickly turns to tears
When selfish motives starve the soul.

The few who choose the narrow road
Lean on the Master's hand.
No matter what the day brings,
PEACE is released within.

Mounting up on eagle's wings
Takes them to higher ground,
Where renewed spirits find their place,
Secure in the great I AM.

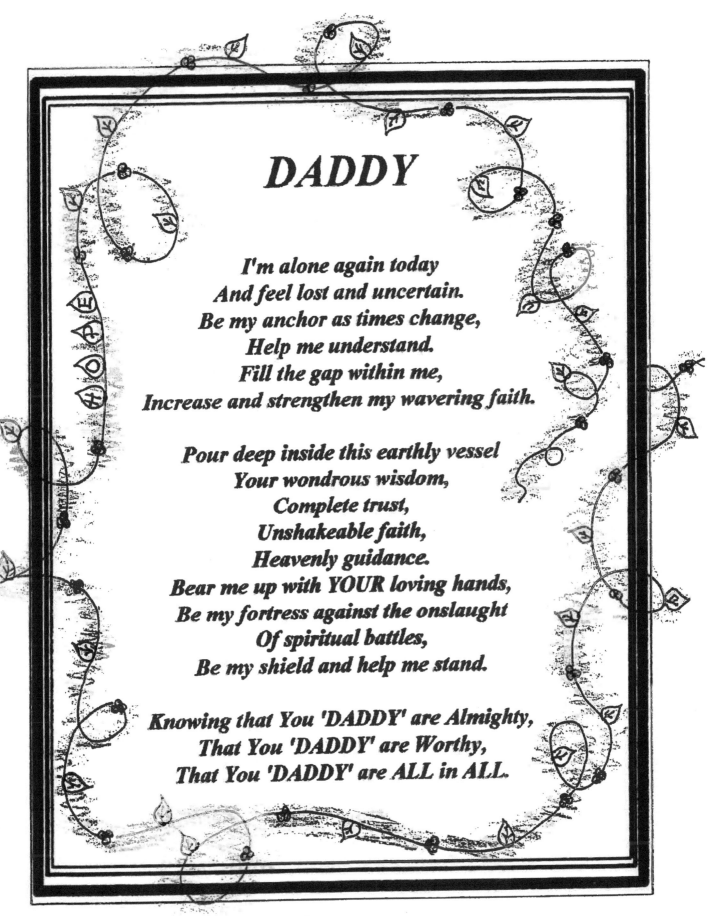

DADDY

I'm alone again today
And feel lost and uncertain.
Be my anchor as times change,
Help me understand.
Fill the gap within me,
Increase and strengthen my wavering faith.

Pour deep inside this earthly vessel
Your wondrous wisdom,
Complete trust,
Unshakeable faith,
Heavenly guidance.
Bear me up with YOUR loving hands,
Be my fortress against the onslaught
Of spiritual battles,
Be my shield and help me stand.

Knowing that You 'DADDY' are Almighty,
That You 'DADDY' are Worthy,
That You 'DADDY' are ALL in ALL.

6.

DREAMS

Dreams deposited in the heart
Sustain the soul within,
Given by GOD to HIS children,
To bring Life to the eyes
Of CHRIST's body.

Satan cannot steal
That which has taken hold,
For dreams inspire mortal man
To grasp the impossible,
Snatching away defeat
From the principalities, powers of darkness.

GOD's Glory will reign,
As man's visions take feet.
Lifted by the SPIRIT,
Supported by Faith,
Dreams become reality.

BEGINNINGS

A new year,

A new beginning,

What lies ahead, LORD?

Struggles, growth, wisdom, love.

Struggles

To know Your will in all,

To overcome self-pity, temptations

To conquer doubts, fears, losses,

To still the restless evil, the tongue.

Growth

To grow through discipline,

Through sacrifice, moderation, surrender,

To rely on FAITH and the WORD,

To walk behind, beside the MASTER.

Wisdom

Given freely without doubts,

Through struggles, one grows,

With growth comes wisdom,

With wisdom comes love.

Love

The total surrender to ABBA

All fear cast aside

Willing to step out in faith,

A vessel overflowing with CHARITY.

8.

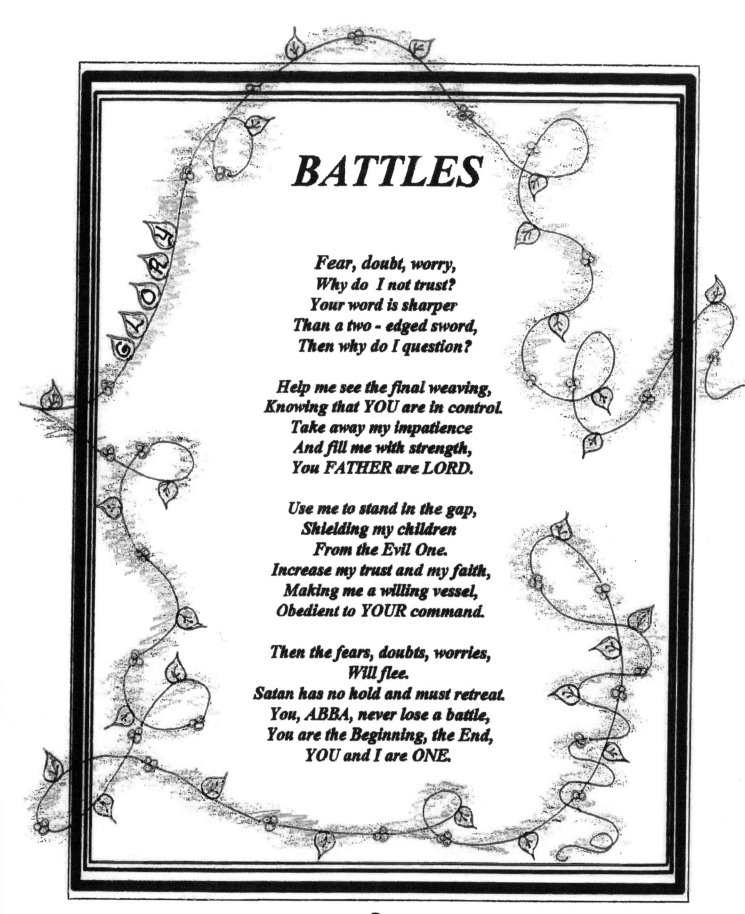

BATTLES

Fear, doubt, worry,
Why do I not trust?
Your word is sharper
Than a two - edged sword,
Then why do I question?

Help me see the final weaving,
Knowing that YOU are in control.
Take away my impatience
And fill me with strength,
You FATHER are LORD.

Use me to stand in the gap,
Shielding my children
From the Evil One.
Increase my trust and my faith,
Making me a willing vessel,
Obedient to YOUR command.

Then the fears, doubts, worries,
Will flee.
Satan has no hold and must retreat.
You, ABBA, never lose a battle,
You are the Beginning, the End,
YOU and I are ONE.

GOD'S ANSWER

My children, hear my cry,
Why have you deserted me?
Why have you stolen from me?
Where is your love?
Where is your loyalty?
Would I rob you?
Would I steal from you?
Is not my Word true?
Am I not faithful to fulfill it?
Yet, you say I cannot be trusted,
That I break my covenant.

Beware my little ones,
I AM does not lie!
You are the ones who break faith,
You are the ones who deceive,
You scheme and fraud one another
And yet ask, "Where are the blessings?"
First humble yourself,
Make peace with your neighbor,
Turn back to me and repent.
Then I'll hear from heaven
And stay MY wrath.

10.

HOLY

When blessings come pouring down upon our earthly tents, it is easy to praise the Most High Creator. However, when droughts come and the tempest roars, it is then our praises need to swell. Heartfelt songs of thanksgiving to the Great I AM unlock heaven's gates and allow the sweet fragrance of God's grace and mercy to flood our lives, renew our strength, and restore our souls.

Obedience comes with a price - sacrifice. We give up our hurts, our pains and lay them at the feet of Jesus when we lift our voices in adoration. "Let us continually offer to God a sacrifice of praise - the fruit of lips that confess His name." Heb. 13:15

Part II of my book is entitled "HE IS". God is found in every aspect of our lives, from the first blade of grass to the last withered leaf that clings to the vine. GOD IS!

Let the name of the lord be praised, both now and forevermore. From the rising of the sun to the place where it sets, the name of the Lord is to be praised.

Psalm 113:2-3

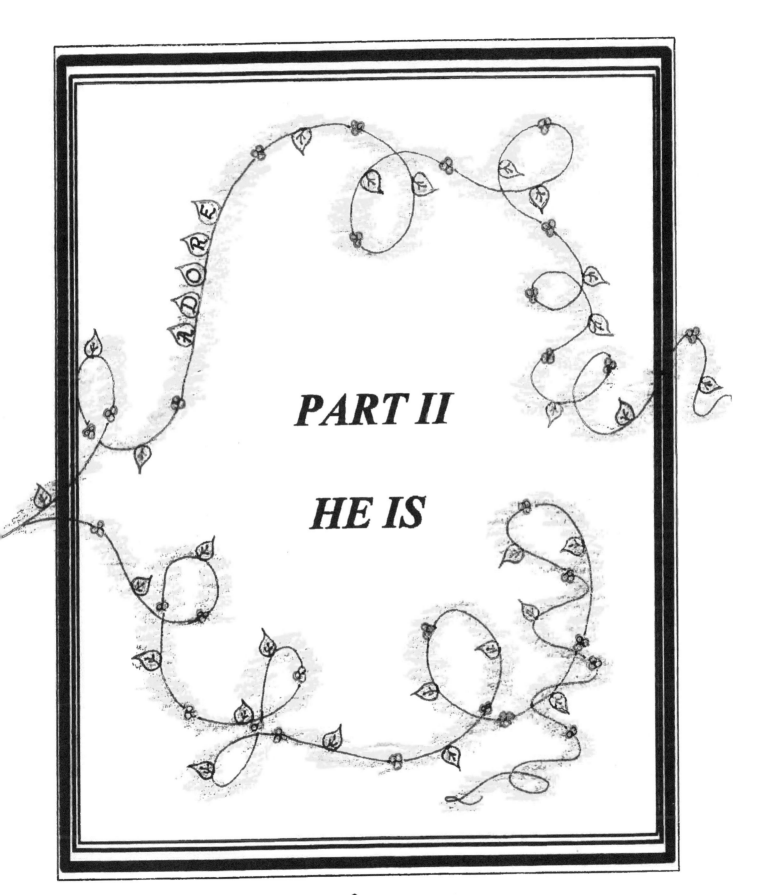

PART II

HE IS

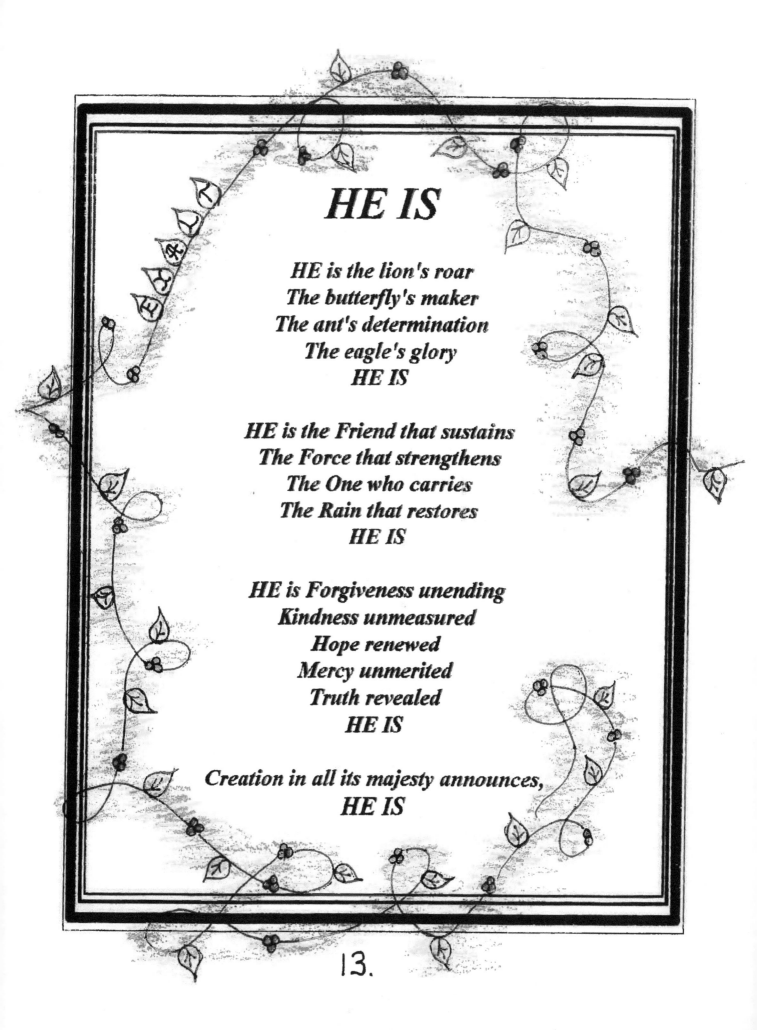

HE IS

HE is the lion's roar
The butterfly's maker
The ant's determination
The eagle's glory
HE IS

HE is the Friend that sustains
The Force that strengthens
The One who carries
The Rain that restores
HE IS

HE is Forgiveness unending
Kindness unmeasured
Hope renewed
Mercy unmerited
Truth revealed
HE IS

Creation in all its majesty announces,
HE IS

13.

GOD'S FAITHFULNESS

Winds come and winds go,
But the Word of the LORD
Is steadfast and unwavering.

HIS pinions will keep you
High above the tempest
Where no principality, no power
Can touch HIS anointed.

HE will bear you up
On eagle's wings
To soar to heights
Unknown to man,
Immersed in the SON's rays.

14.

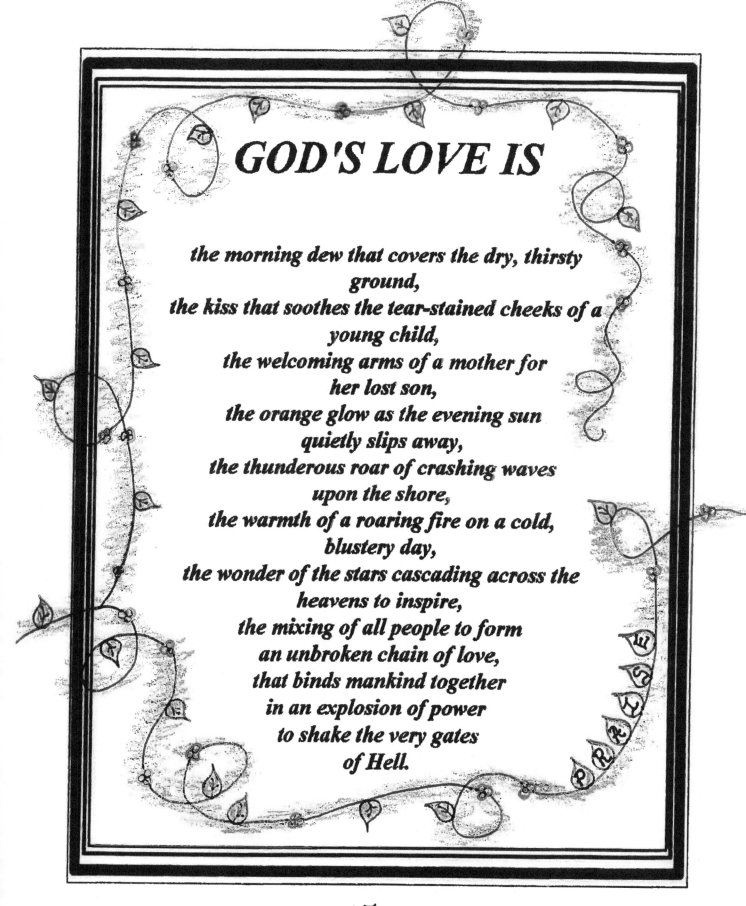

GOD'S LOVE IS

the morning dew that covers the dry, thirsty
ground,
the kiss that soothes the tear-stained cheeks of a
young child,
the welcoming arms of a mother for
her lost son,
the orange glow as the evening sun
quietly slips away,
the thunderous roar of crashing waves
upon the shore,
the warmth of a roaring fire on a cold,
blustery day,
the wonder of the stars cascading across the
heavens to inspire,
the mixing of all people to form
an unbroken chain of love,
that binds mankind together
in an explosion of power
to shake the very gates
of Hell.

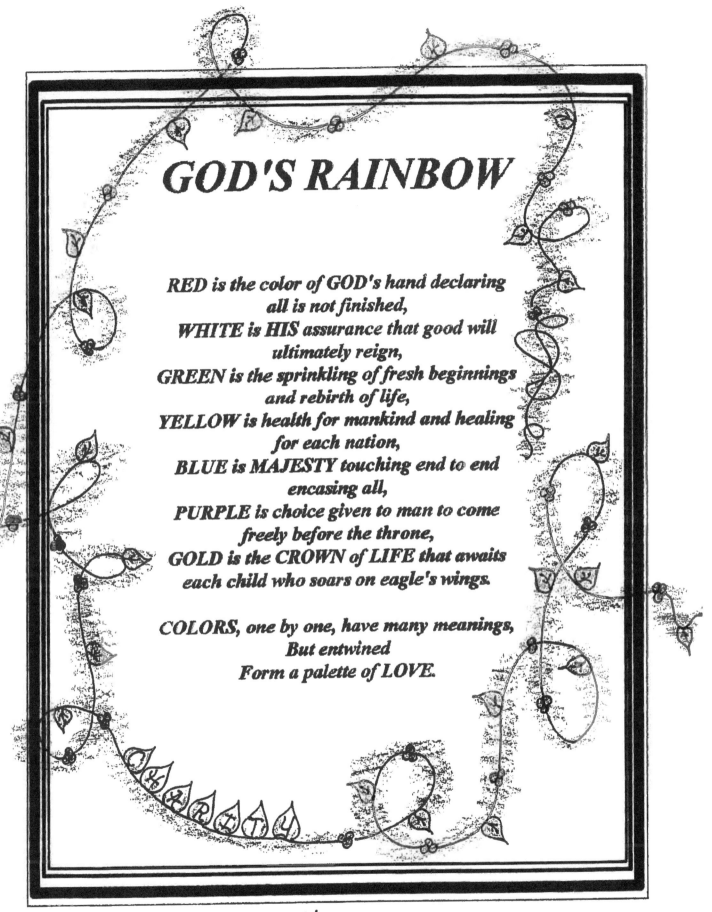

GOD'S RAINBOW

RED is the color of GOD's hand declaring
all is not finished,
WHITE is HIS assurance that good will
ultimately reign,
GREEN is the sprinkling of fresh beginnings
and rebirth of life,
YELLOW is health for mankind and healing
for each nation,
BLUE is MAJESTY touching end to end
encasing all,
PURPLE is choice given to man to come
freely before the throne,
GOLD is the CROWN of LIFE that awaits
each child who soars on eagle's wings.

COLORS, one by one, have many meanings,
But entwined
Form a palette of LOVE.

16.

FRIENDS

The gift of friendship
Is a priceless jewel,
Kissed by the MASTER's hand,
Given to us
To be nourished, honored, shared.

Knowing GOD's touch
Has brought you friends,
Is joy beyond measure.

As the dawn breaks forth
Afresh each day,
So friendship
Brings renewed hope
Of the day to come.

THE POWER OF LOVE

The warmth of a bearskin rug,
The contentment of a roaring fire,
The laughter of a small child,
The soft drumming of rain above,
All cannot express
The encompassing LOVE
GOD has for HIS children.

Released anew each day,
The FATHER's Love
Enfolds around each one
To protect, caress, heal,
All that has been lost or stolen.

18.

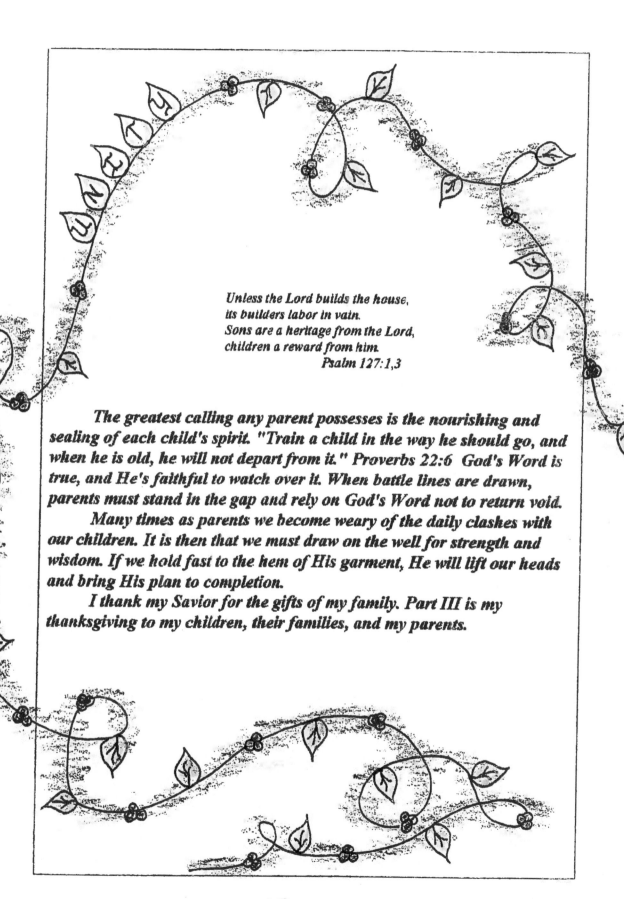

Unless the Lord builds the house,
its builders labor in vain.
Sons are a heritage from the Lord,
children a reward from him.
Psalm 127:1,3

The greatest calling any parent possesses is the nourishing and sealing of each child's spirit. "Train a child in the way he should go, and when he is old, he will not depart from it." Proverbs 22:6 God's Word is true, and He's faithful to watch over it. When battle lines are drawn, parents must stand in the gap and rely on God's Word not to return void.

Many times as parents we become weary of the daily clashes with our children. It is then that we must draw on the well for strength and wisdom. If we hold fast to the hem of His garment, He will lift our heads and bring His plan to completion.

I thank my Savior for the gifts of my family. Part III is my thanksgiving to my children, their families, and my parents.

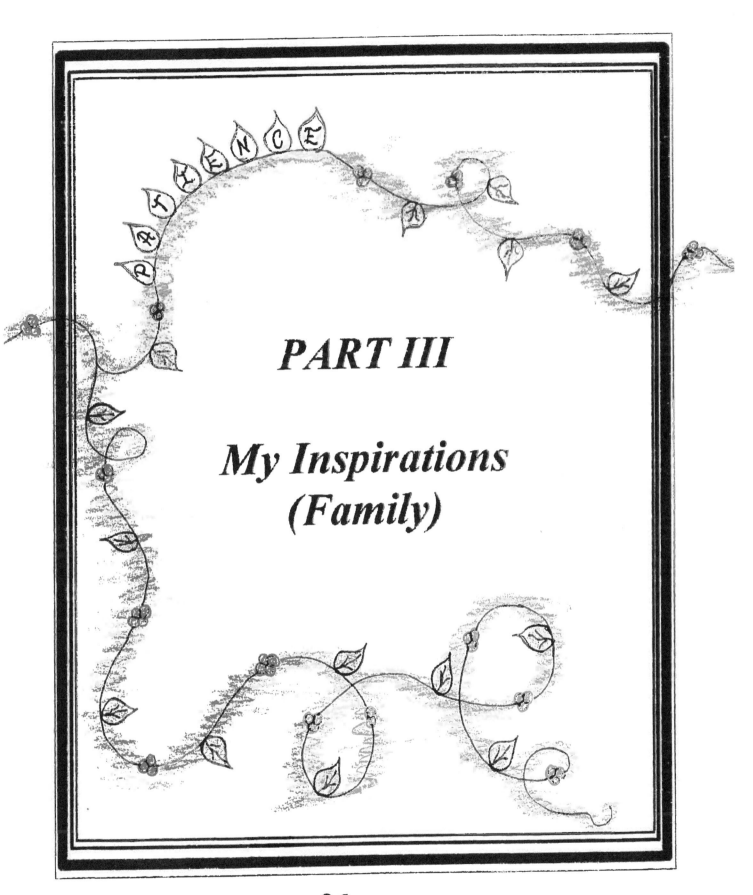

PART III

My Inspirations
(Family)

THANK YOU, ABBA

As I lie in bed

Beneath YOUR loving gaze,

I think how Blessed

My life has suddenly become.

Before I had time

To ask for heavenly wisdom,

Blessings too beautiful to behold

Came pouring down upon my tent.

My children, LORD,

Ever so quietly began to grow

In knowledge and love

Too wondrous to understand.

As I ponder the beginning

Of each new day

I know YOU'll lead me

To horizons beyond my dreams.

And when I close my eyes this night,

I want to say to you, FATHER,

Thank YOU for the Gift of Life.

21.

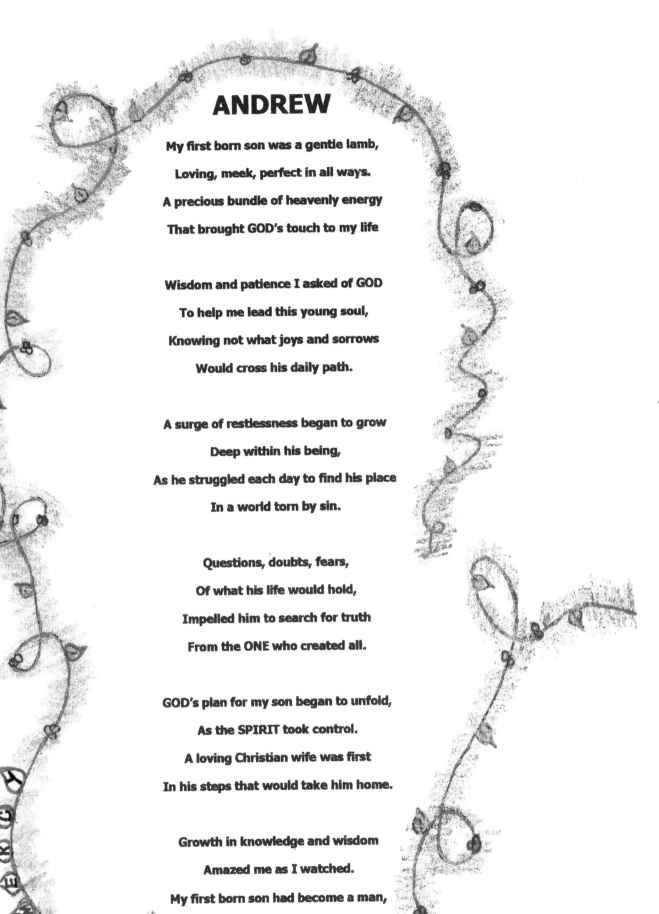

ANDREW

My first born son was a gentle lamb,

Loving, meek, perfect in all ways.

A precious bundle of heavenly energy

That brought GOD's touch to my life

Wisdom and patience I asked of GOD

To help me lead this young soul,

Knowing not what joys and sorrows

Would cross his daily path.

A surge of restlessness began to grow

Deep within his being,

As he struggled each day to find his place

In a world torn by sin.

Questions, doubts, fears,

Of what his life would hold,

Impelled him to search for truth

From the ONE who created all.

GOD's plan for my son began to unfold,

As the SPIRIT took control.

A loving Christian wife was first

In his steps that would take him home.

Growth in knowledge and wisdom

Amazed me as I watched.

My first born son had become a man,

Ready to take his stand.

22.

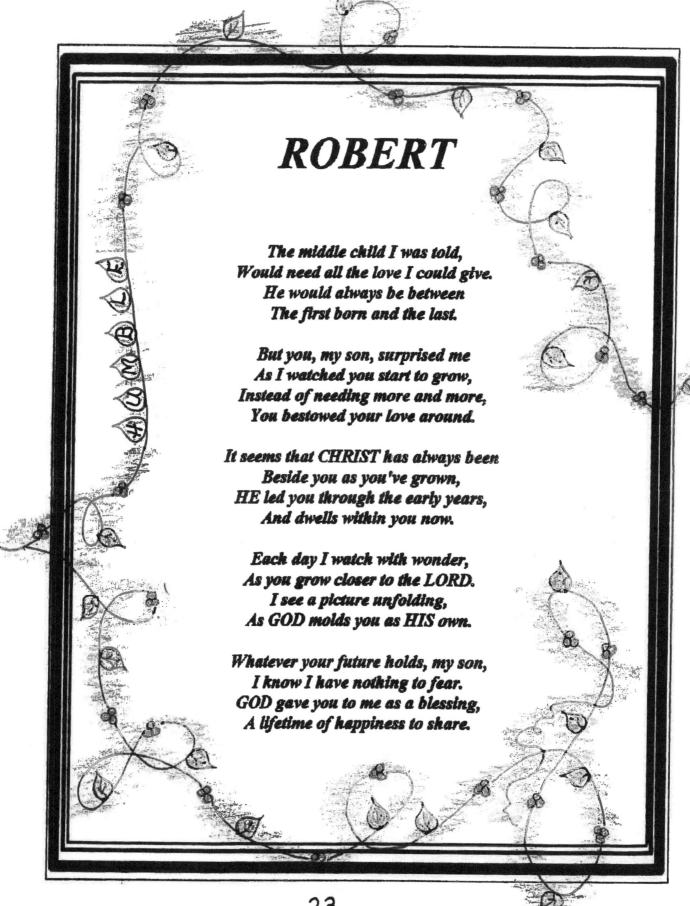

ROBERT

The middle child I was told,
Would need all the love I could give.
He would always be between
The first born and the last.

But you, my son, surprised me
As I watched you start to grow,
Instead of needing more and more,
You bestowed your love around.

It seems that CHRIST has always been
Beside you as you've grown,
HE led you through the early years,
And dwells within you now.

Each day I watch with wonder,
As you grow closer to the LORD.
I see a picture unfolding,
As GOD molds you as HIS own.

Whatever your future holds, my son,
I know I have nothing to fear.
GOD gave you to me as a blessing,
A lifetime of happiness to share.

23.

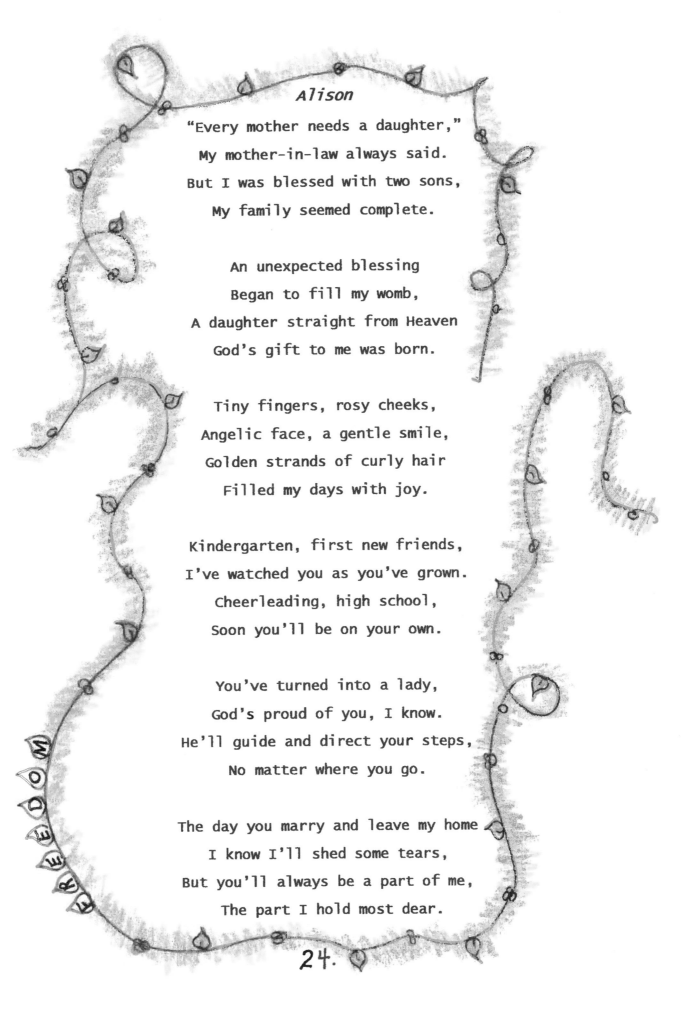

Alison

"Every mother needs a daughter,"
My mother-in-law always said.
But I was blessed with two sons,
My family seemed complete.

An unexpected blessing
Began to fill my womb,
A daughter straight from Heaven
God's gift to me was born.

Tiny fingers, rosy cheeks,
Angelic face, a gentle smile,
Golden strands of curly hair
Filled my days with joy.

Kindergarten, first new friends,
I've watched you as you've grown.
Cheerleading, high school,
Soon you'll be on your own.

You've turned into a lady,
God's proud of you, I know.
He'll guide and direct your steps,
No matter where you go.

The day you marry and leave my home
I know I'll shed some tears,
But you'll always be a part of me,
The part I hold most dear.

Grandchildren

Dreams kissed by the SON
Visions formed by the MASTER's hand,
Molded into precious jewels.

GOD's gifts to us
Each encased with divine talents
To be freely given
To bring laughter, sunshine, rain.

Each child stirs hearts and awakens minds
With childlike faith
To unfold the FATHER's plan.

Unique treasures
Encased with divine love
Shine light through the darkness
Bringing healing to a hurting world.

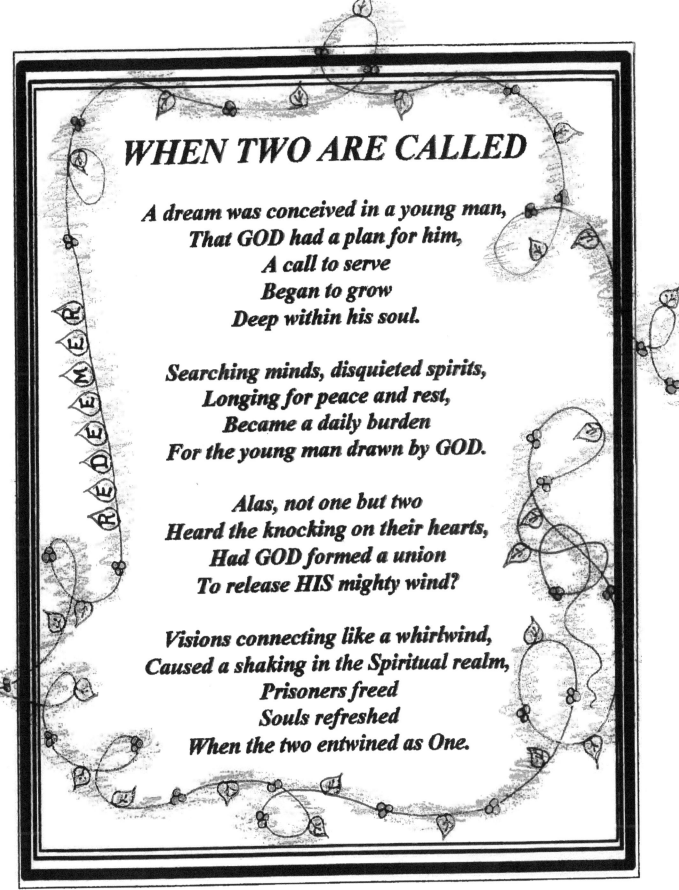

WHEN TWO ARE CALLED

A dream was conceived in a young man,
That GOD had a plan for him,
A call to serve
Began to grow
Deep within his soul.

Searching minds, disquieted spirits,
Longing for peace and rest,
Became a daily burden
For the young man drawn by GOD.

Alas, not one but two
Heard the knocking on their hearts,
Had GOD formed a union
To release HIS mighty wind?

Visions connecting like a whirlwind,
Caused a shaking in the Spiritual realm,
Prisoners freed
Souls refreshed
When the two entwined as One.

STEPHEN

Hand in hand,
One leading, one following,
Through dolls, trains, Howdy Doody,
We grew together.

Day by day
Our spirits joined,
Forming an unbroken chain
That would sustain us
Over distance and time.

Brother and sister,
Side by side,
Spoke to the world
That Love never fails
When ties are entwined.

27.

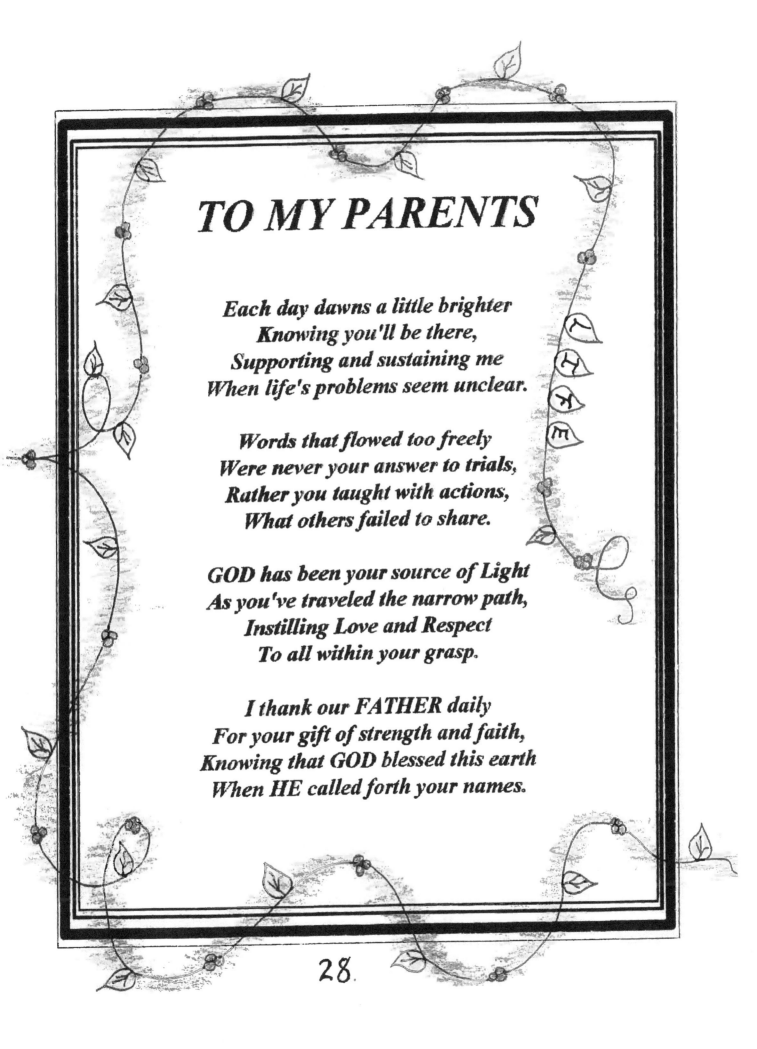

TO MY PARENTS

Each day dawns a little brighter
Knowing you'll be there,
Supporting and sustaining me
When life's problems seem unclear.

Words that flowed too freely
Were never your answer to trials,
Rather you taught with actions,
What others failed to share.

GOD has been your source of Light
As you've traveled the narrow path,
Instilling Love and Respect
To all within your grasp.

I thank our FATHER daily
For your gift of strength and faith,
Knowing that GOD blessed this earth
When HE called forth your names.

One of the joys found in the Christian walk is the unexpected lights that GOD brings into your path. Sometimes, it's a simple smile from a friend that lets you know you're loved; often though, it's the person who anchors you to the vine when your roots seem to be slipping. GOD places each of these lights in your walk to help you grow and to bring you rays of hope for your tomorrows.

Part IV of my book is designed to introduce you to the lights that a loving FATHER has placed before me. Each person has been used to teach me how to live, how to dream, and how to walk. They are the heroes that answered when GOD called.

I no longer call you servants, because a servant does not know his master's business. Instead, I have called you friends, for everything that I have learned from my Father, I have made known to you. You did not choose me, but I chose you and appointed you to go and bear fruit – fruit that will last. Then the Father will give you whatever you ask in my name.

John 15:15-16

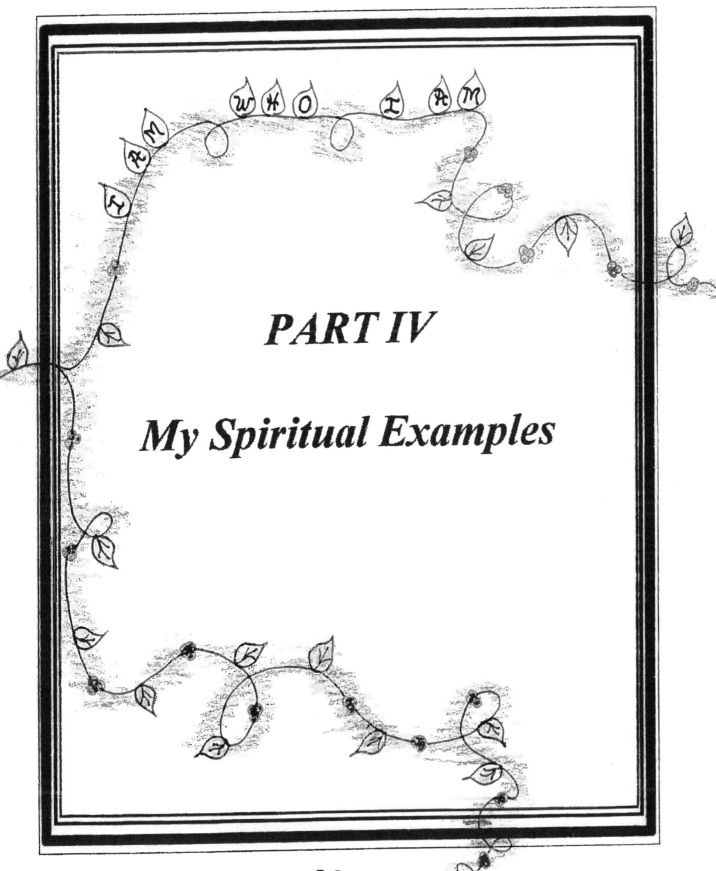

PART IV

My Spiritual Examples

A Voice Proclaiming Freedom

God called,

I answered

What Lord?

Proclaim, Proclaim

Freedom, Liberty, Righteousness,

Obedience

Joyce Meyer

FREEDOM

To be one's self

To be led by the SPIRIT,

To allow others the GRACE

To be themselves.

LIBERTY

To be humble before men,

To wait patiently for GOD"s move,

To show mercy and forgiveness.

RIGHTEOUSNESS

To know you are right with GOD,

To know you are hidden in that secret place,

To know you tread where angels dare not go.

OBEDIENCE

To understand victory comes through obeying,

With freedom comes responsibility,

With righteousness comes surrender.

Well done

Thy good and faithful servant.

31.

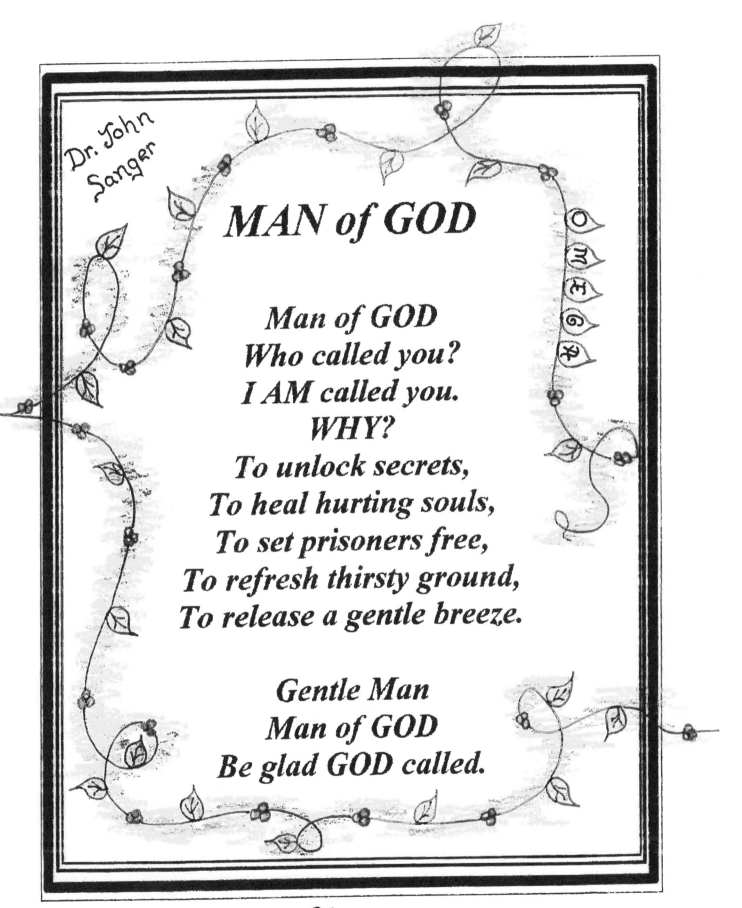

Dr. John
Sanger

MAN of GOD

Man of GOD
Who called you?
I AM called you.
WHY?
To unlock secrets,
To heal hurting souls,
To set prisoners free,
To refresh thirsty ground,
To release a gentle breeze.

Gentle Man
Man of GOD
Be glad GOD called.

O
M
E
G
A

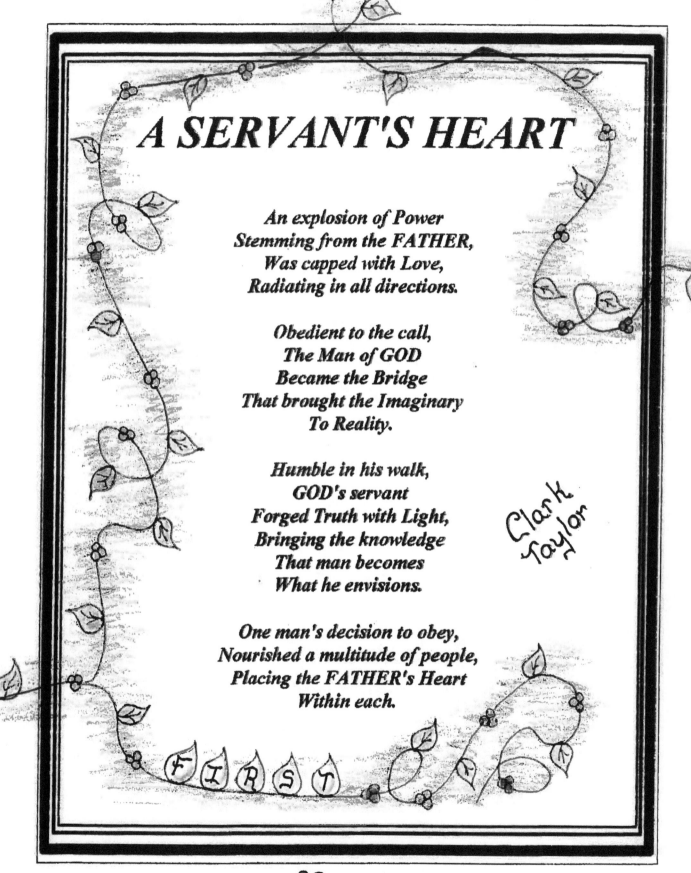

A SERVANT'S HEART

An explosion of Power
Stemming from the FATHER,
Was capped with Love,
Radiating in all directions.

Obedient to the call,
The Man of GOD
Became the Bridge
That brought the Imaginary
To Reality.

Humble in his walk,
GOD's servant
Forged Truth with Light,
Bringing the knowledge
That man becomes
What he envisions.

One man's decision to obey,
Nourished a multitude of people,
Placing the FATHER's Heart
Within each.

Clark Taylor

FIRST

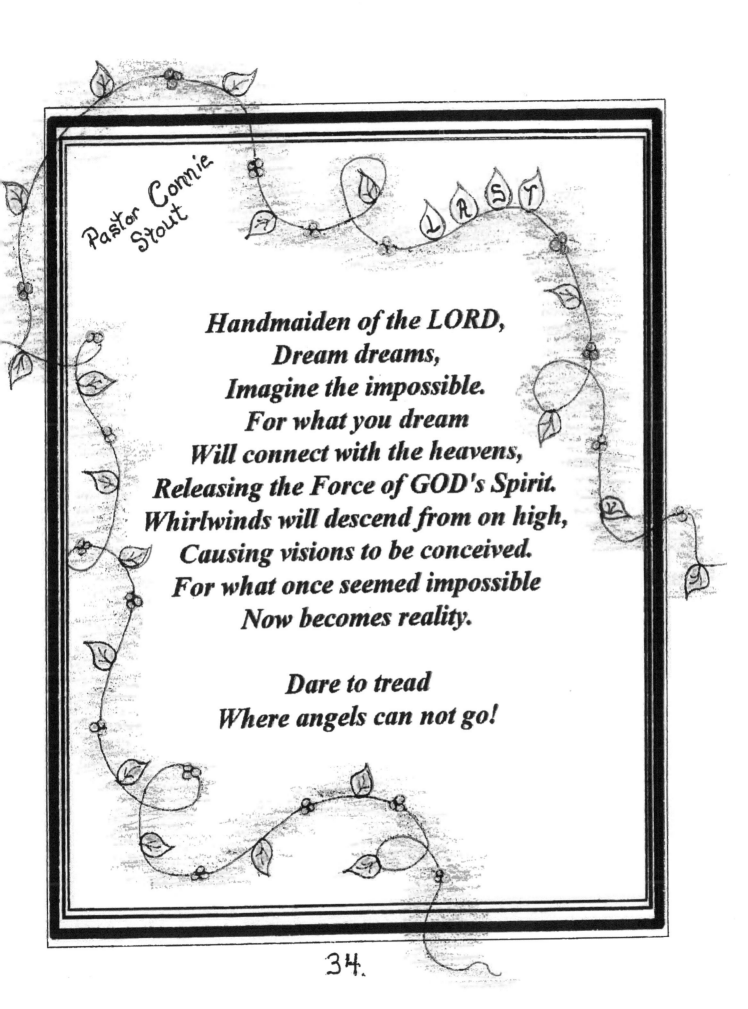

Pastor Connie
Stout

LAST

Handmaiden of the LORD,
Dream dreams,
Imagine the impossible.
For what you dream
Will connect with the heavens,
Releasing the Force of GOD's Spirit.
Whirlwinds will descend from on high,
Causing visions to be conceived.
For what once seemed impossible
Now becomes reality.

Dare to tread
Where angels can not go!

34.

Pastor John Stout

Hear Ye, Hear Ye,

Son of Man
A Day is Coming
When the Glory Of the LORD
Will Be Revealed.
Stand Back and Watch
The Manifestation of the SPIRIT.

Behold I Come in a New Way,
The Heavens Will Part
And My Anointing Will Be Poured Out
Upon My Chosen.
For the Old Has Passed Away,
A New Day Has Dawned!

BEGINNING

35.

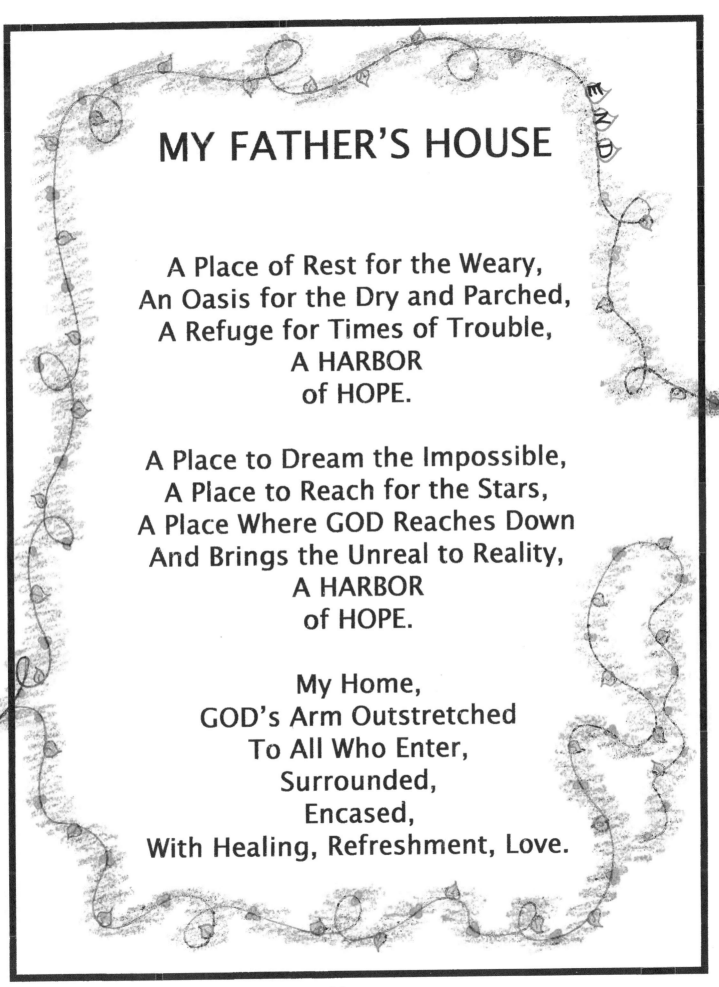

MY FATHER'S HOUSE

A Place of Rest for the Weary,
An Oasis for the Dry and Parched,
A Refuge for Times of Trouble,
A HARBOR
of HOPE.

A Place to Dream the Impossible,
A Place to Reach for the Stars,
A Place Where GOD Reaches Down
And Brings the Unreal to Reality,
A HARBOR
of HOPE.

My Home,
GOD's Arm Outstretched
To All Who Enter,
Surrounded,
Encased,
With Healing, Refreshment, Love.

A Dear Friend

DOUG

The day you were created
GOD had a masterful plan,
To bring sunshine to earth,
To make each day a little brighter.

Obedient to the call,
Your laughter sparked the heavens
And set a flame in men
That exploded into unspeakable joy,
Causing darkness to diminish.

A smile upon your face,
Spread rainbows of happiness
To all you touched,
Rippling across the oceans
Of many human hearts.

Now the heavens rejoice
Singing and recanting your praise,
Filling the firmament with gladness,
That another son is on his way.

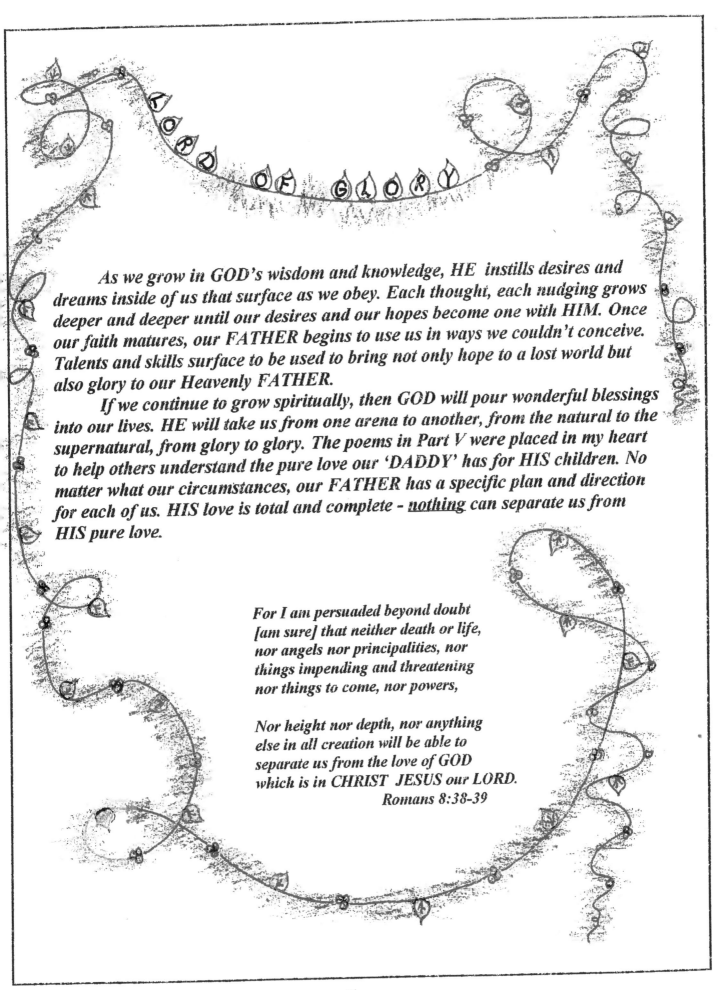

LORD OF GLORY

As we grow in GOD's wisdom and knowledge, HE instills desires and dreams inside of us that surface as we obey. Each thought, each nudging grows deeper and deeper until our desires and our hopes become one with HIM. Once our faith matures, our FATHER begins to use us in ways we couldn't conceive. Talents and skills surface to be used to bring not only hope to a lost world but also glory to our Heavenly FATHER.

If we continue to grow spiritually, then GOD will pour wonderful blessings into our lives. HE will take us from one arena to another, from the natural to the supernatural, from glory to glory. The poems in Part V were placed in my heart to help others understand the pure love our 'DADDY' has for HIS children. No matter what our circumstances, our FATHER has a specific plan and direction for each of us. HIS love is total and complete - nothing can separate us from HIS pure love.

For I am persuaded beyond doubt
[am sure] that neither death or life,
nor angels nor principalities, nor
things impending and threatening
nor things to come, nor powers,

Nor height nor depth, nor anything
else in all creation will be able to
separate us from the love of GOD
which is in CHRIST JESUS our LORD.
Romans 8:38-39

PART V

Truth

THE WORD

The Word is the essence of my being.
When spoken forth,
It penetrates the misty darkness
With piercing light,
Which illuminates the cloak
That covers my desire.

Once spoken,
God's Word cannot return empty,
For truth always manifests light,
Even in the darkest web of our soul.

God gave man the Master Key to Life.
When used with the locks
Of forgiveness and love,
God's Word opens Heaven's doors,
Revealing treasures and blessings
Kept in store for each child
Since the creation of time.

JESUS

PRAISE

Storm clouds gather
As GOD's people begin to praise,
Shouts of Hallelujah,
Announcing freedom, are raised.

A swell of thanksgiving
Ascends to Heaven's gate,
Releasing GOD's power
And rekindling man's faith.

Shackles crumble, one by one,
As the voice of GOD's children
Proclaim, "Liberty is won!"

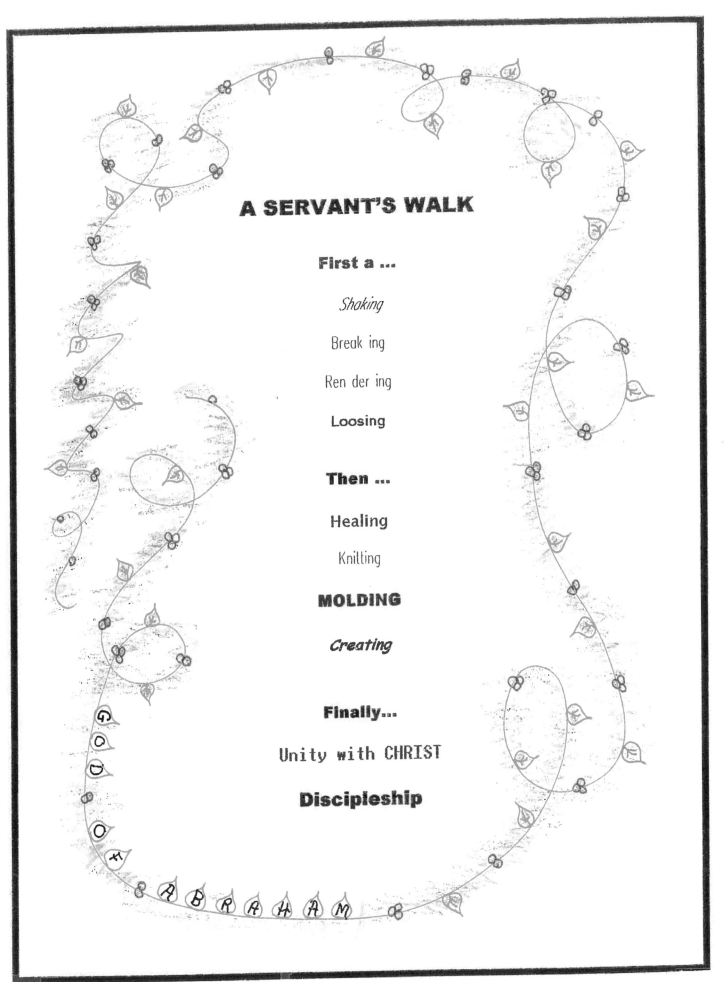

A SERVANT'S WALK

First a ...

Shaking

Break ing

Ren der ing

Loosing

Then ...

Healing

Knitting

MOLDING

Creating

Finally...

Unity with CHRIST

Discipleship

GOD OF ABRAHAM

GRACE

My heart, Oh LORD
Cries out to You,
That without Your Grace,
I am as nothing.

Grace stills the tongue,
A restless evil,
Ready to devour a people.

See my weakness, Oh LORD,
Grant me my request.
Give me Grace to conquer
That enemy that lies within.

It's Grace that I need, Oh LORD,
Grace and Mercy.

Then my lips will swell,
Giving forth praise and adoration,
Spewing healing and fresh beginnings,
That mend the broken-hearted.

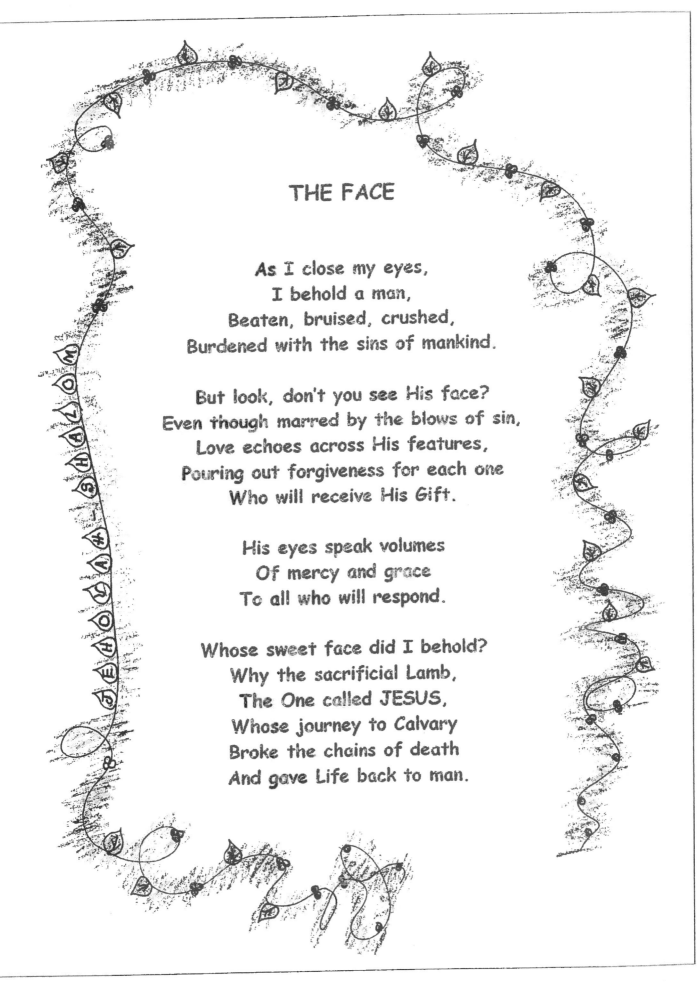

THE FACE

As I close my eyes,
I behold a man,
Beaten, bruised, crushed,
Burdened with the sins of mankind.

But look, don't you see His face?
Even though marred by the blows of sin,
Love echoes across His features,
Pouring out forgiveness for each one
Who will receive His Gift.

His eyes speak volumes
Of mercy and grace
To all who will respond.

Whose sweet face did I behold?
Why the sacrificial Lamb,
The One called JESUS,
Whose journey to Calvary
Broke the chains of death
And gave Life back to man.

Butterfly, butterfly,
From whence did thou come?
"From the hand of the MASTER,
Glorifying HIS all."

Child of GOD, Child of GOD,
From whence did thou come?
"From the dust of the earth,
Given birth when GOD called."

Son of Man, Son of Man,
Why didst thou come?
"To be the Saving Lamb,
Sacrificed for one and all."

Holy Spirit, Holy Spirit,
Why didst thou come?
"To give gifts to men,
To be used when GOD calls."

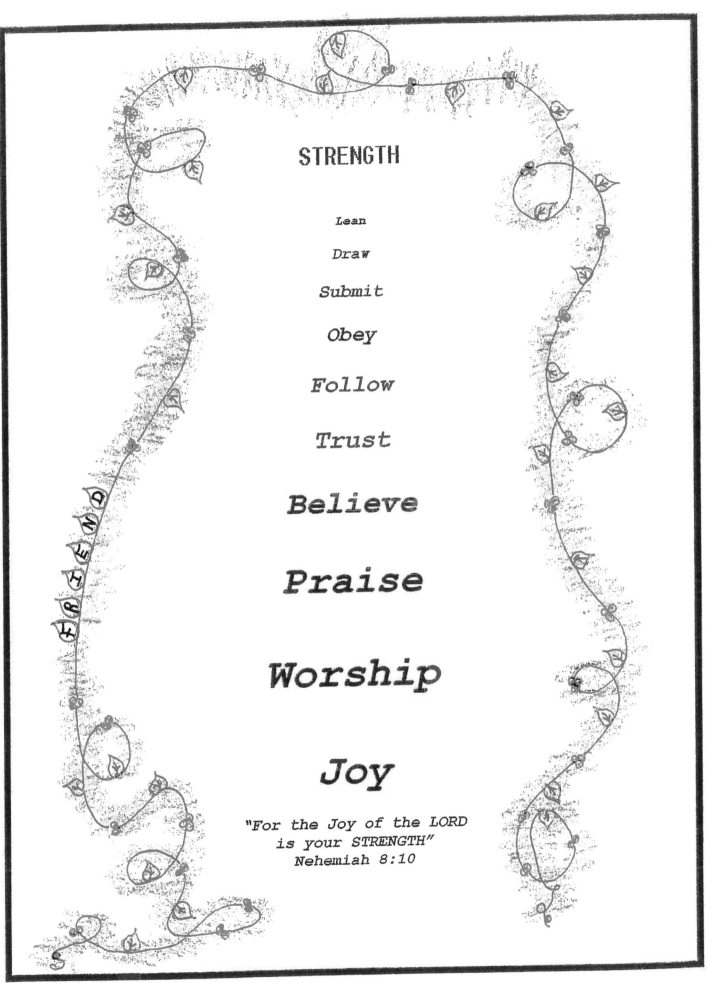

STRENGTH

Lean

Draw

Submit

Obey

Follow

Trust

Believe

Praise

Worship

Joy

"For the Joy of the LORD
is your STRENGTH"
Nehemiah 8:10

46

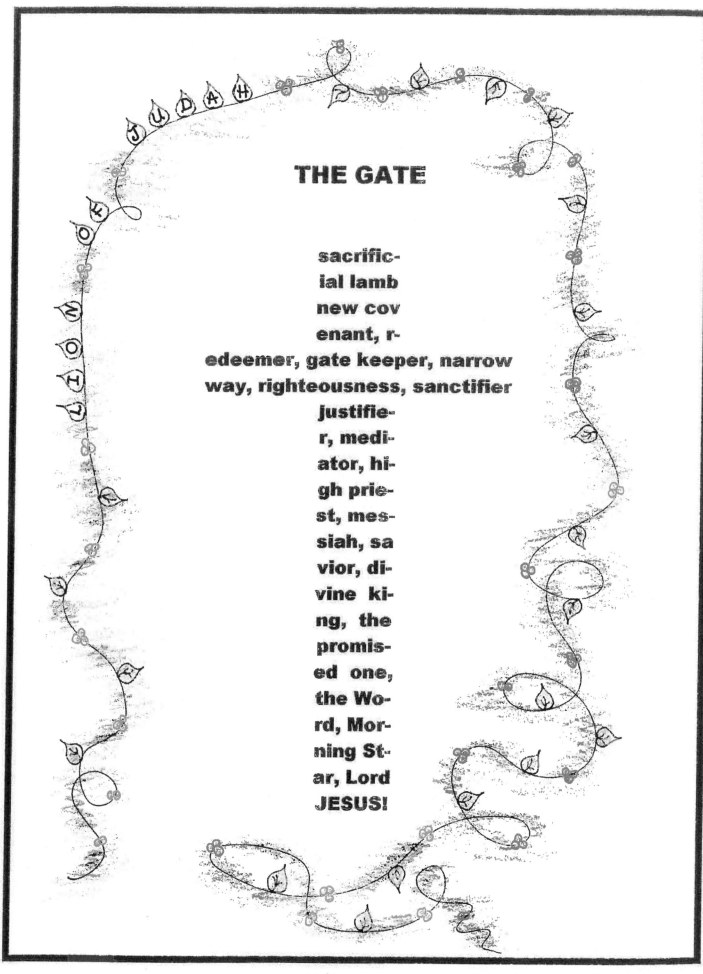

THE GATE

sacrific-
ial lamb
new cov
enant, r-
edeemer, gate keeper, narrow
way, righteousness, sanctifier
justifie-
r, medi-
ator, hi-
gh prie-
st, mes-
siah, sa
vior, di-
vine ki-
ng, the
promis-
ed one,
the Wo-
rd, Mor-
ning St-
ar, Lord
JESUS!

LION OF JUDAH

My heart, Oh LORD, explodes in wonder
At the majesty of your creation.
Every aspect of nature
Cries out YOUR existence.

Trees, reaching toward heaven,
Give wave offerings
To the Most High GOD,
Saying that if mankind refuses,
GOD's creation will still praise.

ENDLESS LOVE

As the heavens encase the universe,
So GOD's love surrounds each child,
Announcing that no deed, no failure,
Can stop the FATHER's passion for His children.

GOD's love is pure,
Like the sweetness of a young child's kiss.
GOD's love is fulfilling,
Like a dream that suddenly becomes real.
GOD's love is redeeming,
Like a lost soul that finds peace.
GOD's love is endless,
Like the stars that cascade across the sky.

Man in his limited knowledge
Cannot fathom so great a Love.
Yet, GOD speaks forth each day
Tiny whispers that say,
"I am here.
Reach for me.
I am LOVE
That will remain."

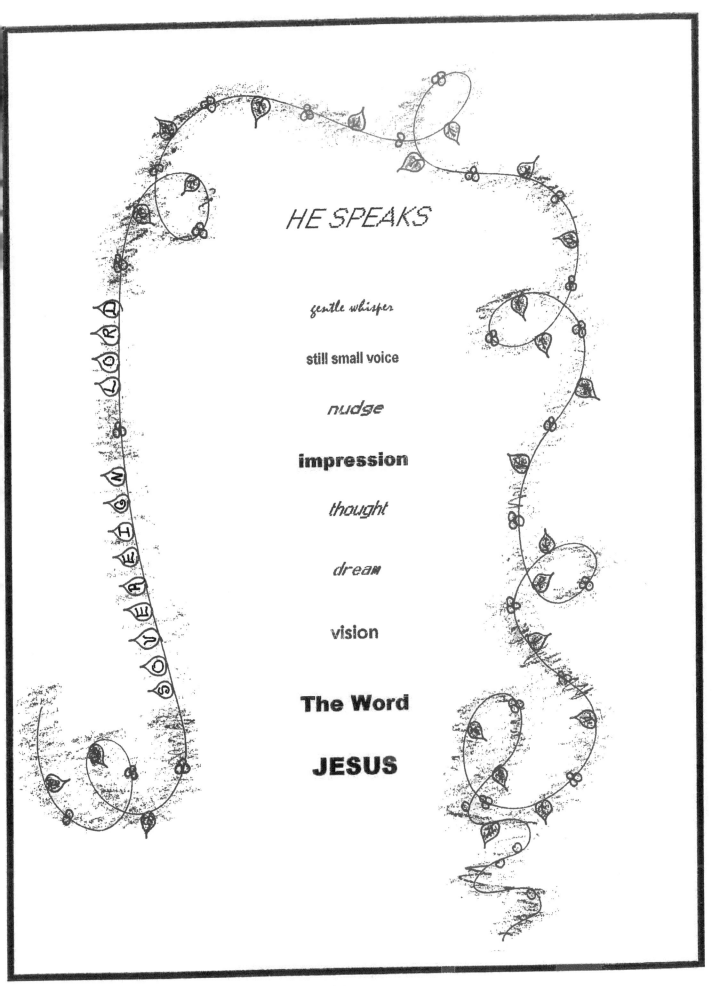

HE SPEAKS

gentle whisper

still small voice

nudge

impression

thought

dream

vision

The Word

JESUS

SOVEREIGN LORD

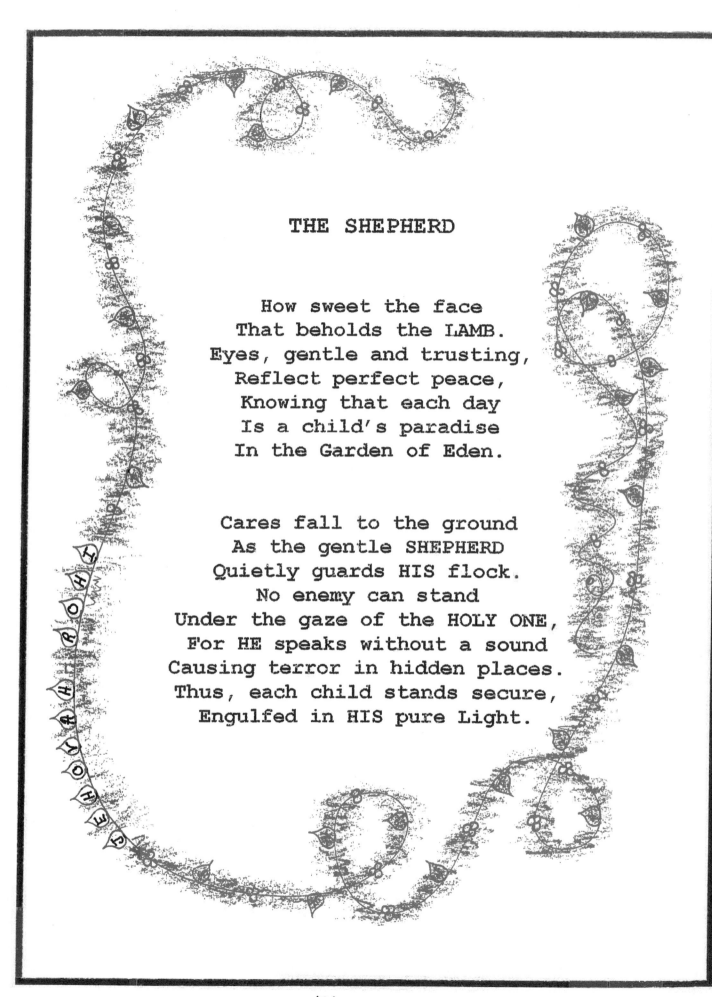

THE SHEPHERD

How sweet the face
That beholds the LAMB.
Eyes, gentle and trusting,
Reflect perfect peace,
Knowing that each day
Is a child's paradise
In the Garden of Eden.

Cares fall to the ground
As the gentle SHEPHERD
Quietly guards HIS flock.
No enemy can stand
Under the gaze of the HOLY ONE,
For HE speaks without a sound
Causing terror in hidden places.
Thus, each child stands secure,
Engulfed in HIS pure Light.

IMMANUEL

A holy hush stirs the air,
A restlessness begins to grow
Deep within the earth.
Animals, sensing an awakening,
Ask the question, "Is it time?"

Nature, travailing in the inner realm,
Bursts forth in majesty and wonder
At the first cry of the newborn child.
Immanuel, 'GOD with us', is born.

A myriad of angels awaken the world
To the arrival of the newborn King.
Redemption has dawned,
Peace will reign,
As GOD's plan for mankind unfolds.

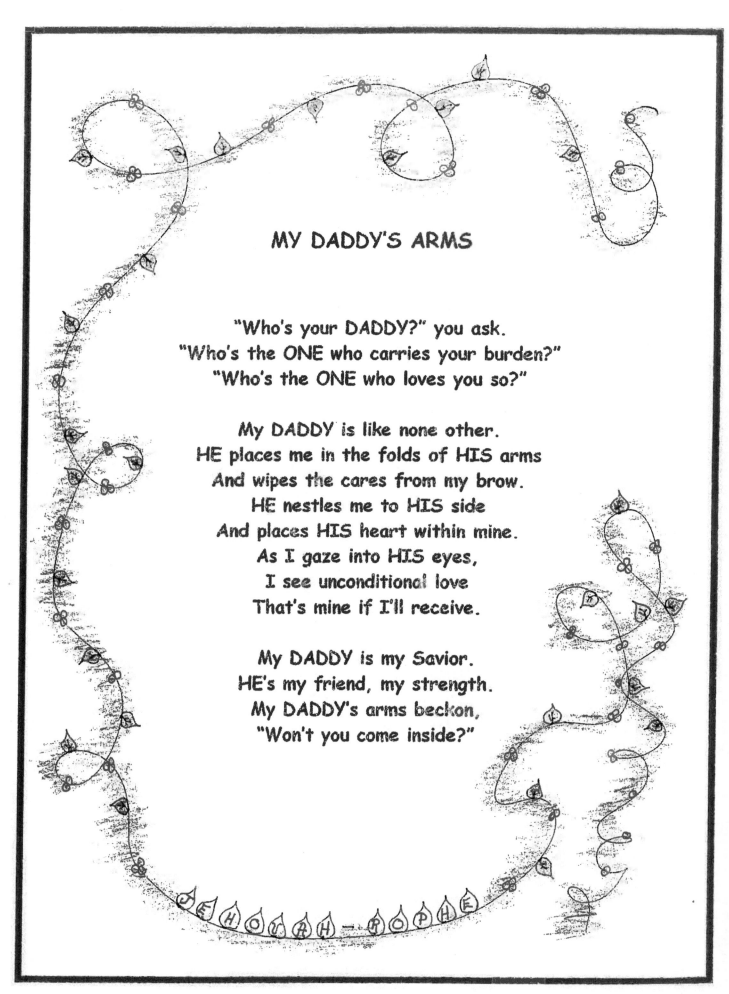

MY DADDY'S ARMS

"Who's your DADDY?" you ask.
"Who's the ONE who carries your burden?"
"Who's the ONE who loves you so?"

My DADDY is like none other.
HE places me in the folds of HIS arms
And wipes the cares from my brow.
HE nestles me to HIS side
And places HIS heart within mine.
As I gaze into HIS eyes,
I see unconditional love
That's mine if I'll receive.

My DADDY is my Savior.
HE's my friend, my strength.
My DADDY's arms beckon,
"Won't you come inside?"

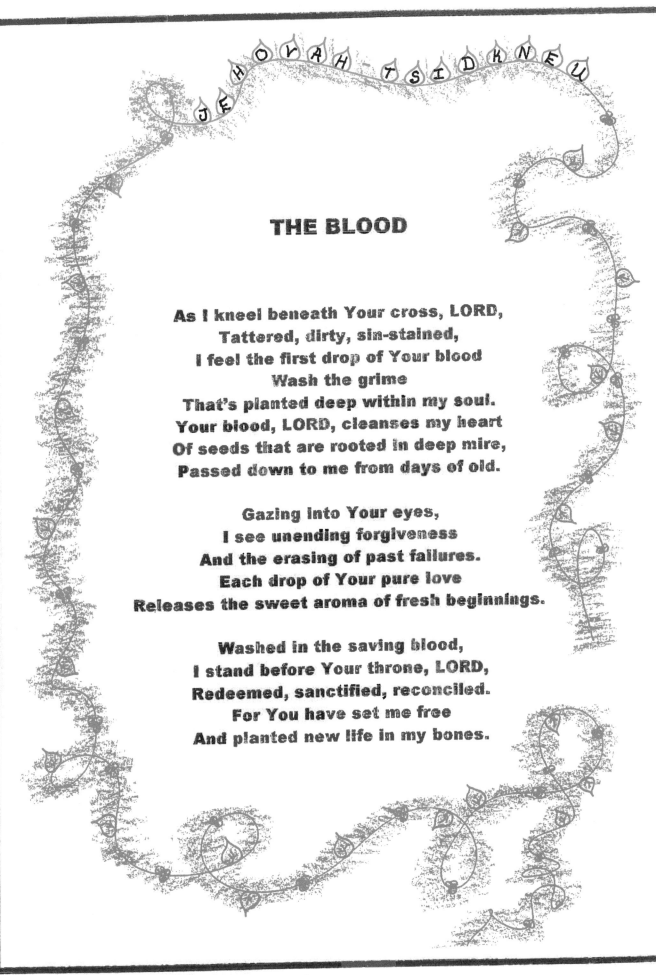

THE BLOOD

As I kneel beneath Your cross, LORD,
Tattered, dirty, sin-stained,
I feel the first drop of Your blood
Wash the grime
That's planted deep within my soul.
Your blood, LORD, cleanses my heart
Of seeds that are rooted in deep mire,
Passed down to me from days of old.

Gazing into Your eyes,
I see unending forgiveness
And the erasing of past failures.
Each drop of Your pure love
Releases the sweet aroma of fresh beginnings.

Washed in the saving blood,
I stand before Your throne, LORD,
Redeemed, sanctified, reconciled.
For You have set me free
And planted new life in my bones.

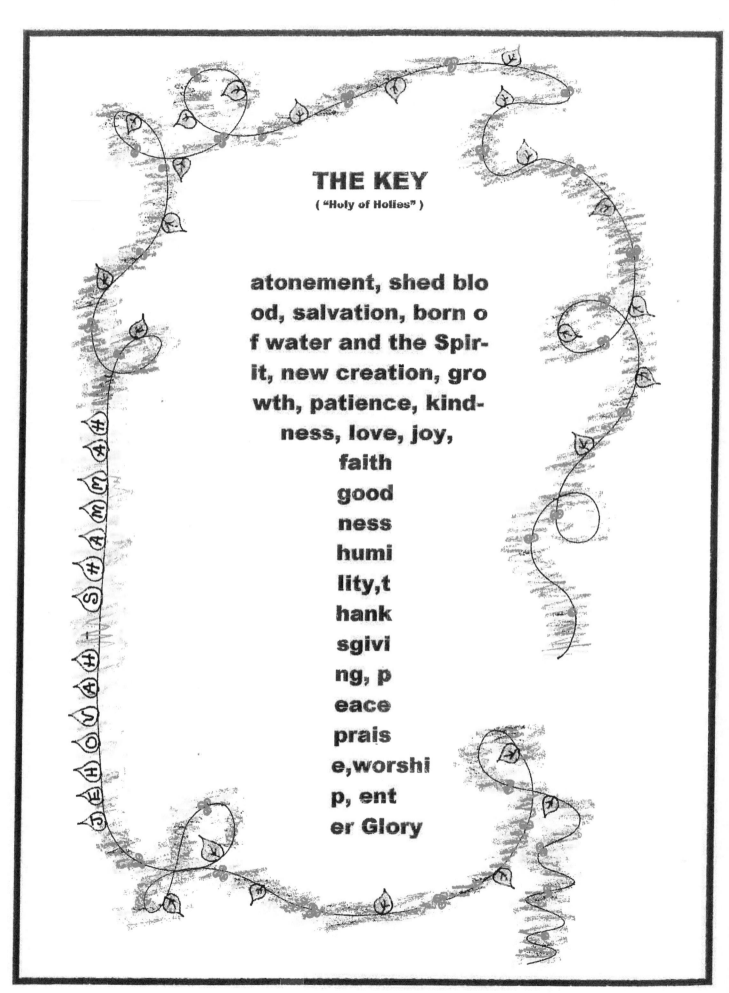

THE KEY
("Holy of Holies")

atonement, shed blo
od, salvation, born o
f water and the Spir-
it, new creation, gro
wth, patience, kind-
ness, love, joy,
faith
good
ness
humi
lity,t
hank
sgivi
ng, p
eace
prais
e,worshi
p, ent
er Glory

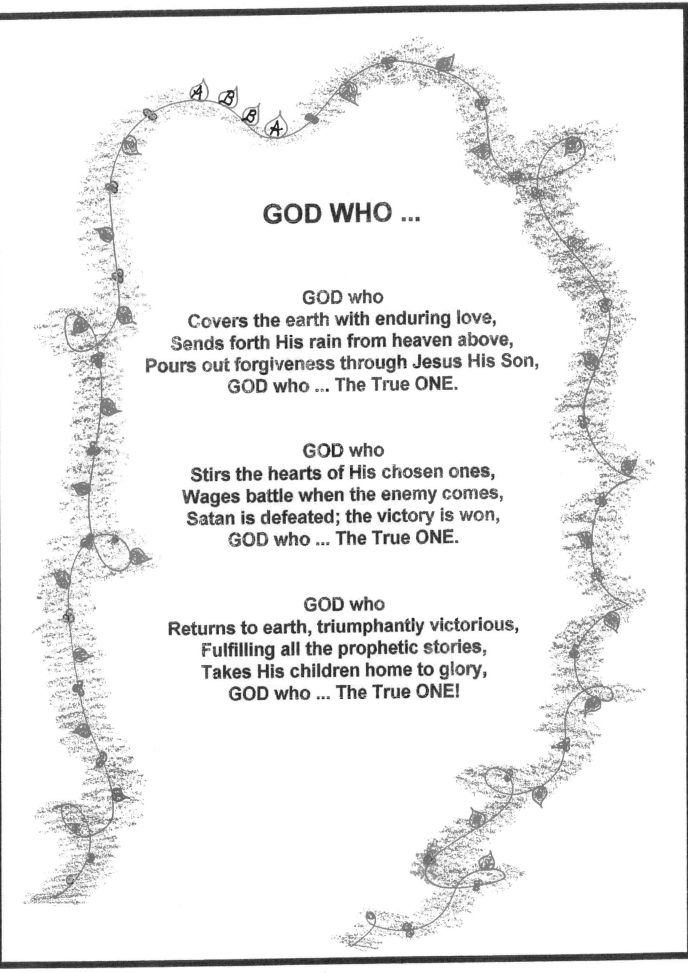

GOD WHO ...

GOD who
Covers the earth with enduring love,
Sends forth His rain from heaven above,
Pours out forgiveness through Jesus His Son,
GOD who ... The True ONE.

GOD who
Stirs the hearts of His chosen ones,
Wages battle when the enemy comes,
Satan is defeated; the victory is won,
GOD who ... The True ONE.

GOD who
Returns to earth, triumphantly victorious,
Fulfilling all the prophetic stories,
Takes His children home to glory,
GOD who ... The True ONE!

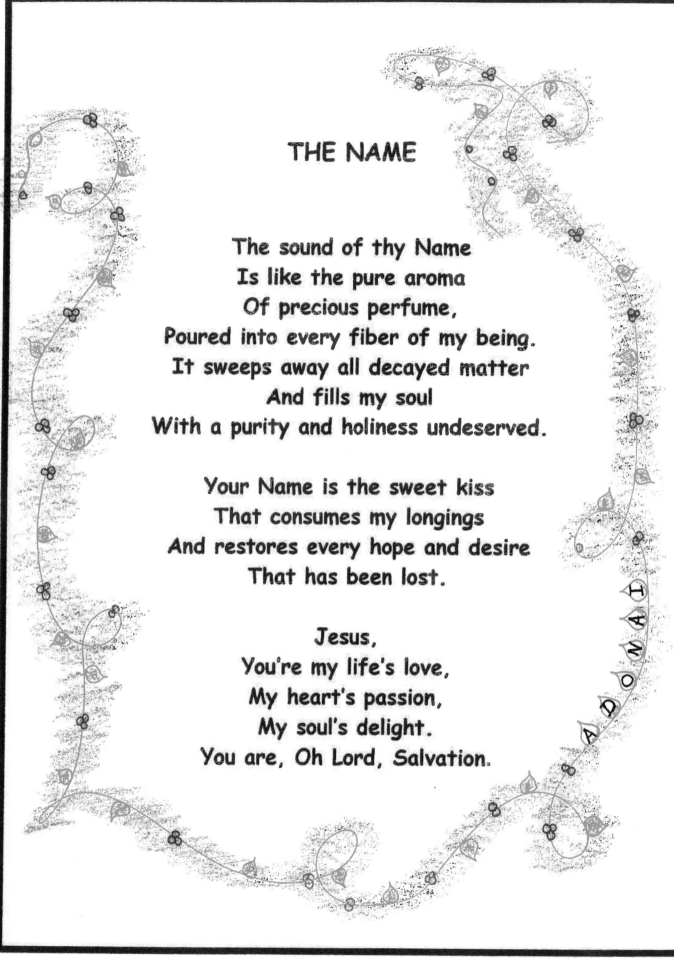

THE NAME

The sound of thy Name
Is like the pure aroma
Of precious perfume,
Poured into every fiber of my being.
It sweeps away all decayed matter
And fills my soul
With a purity and holiness undeserved.

Your Name is the sweet kiss
That consumes my longings
And restores every hope and desire
That has been lost.

Jesus,
You're my life's love,
My heart's passion,
My soul's delight.
You are, Oh Lord, Salvation.

GROWTH

As the spring rains
Clean and refresh the earth,
So God's Son
Cleanses man of his impurities.
Layer by layer
Sin is removed,
Leaving new birth
And fresh beginnings.

If man stays immersed in his Father,
Then growth is continual.
New seeds sprout daily
As water from Heaven
Floods the soul of man.

Satan tries to plant umbrellas
In man's field,
But the power of God's Word
Goes forth like a torrent,
Destroying everything
That brings harm to man's seed.

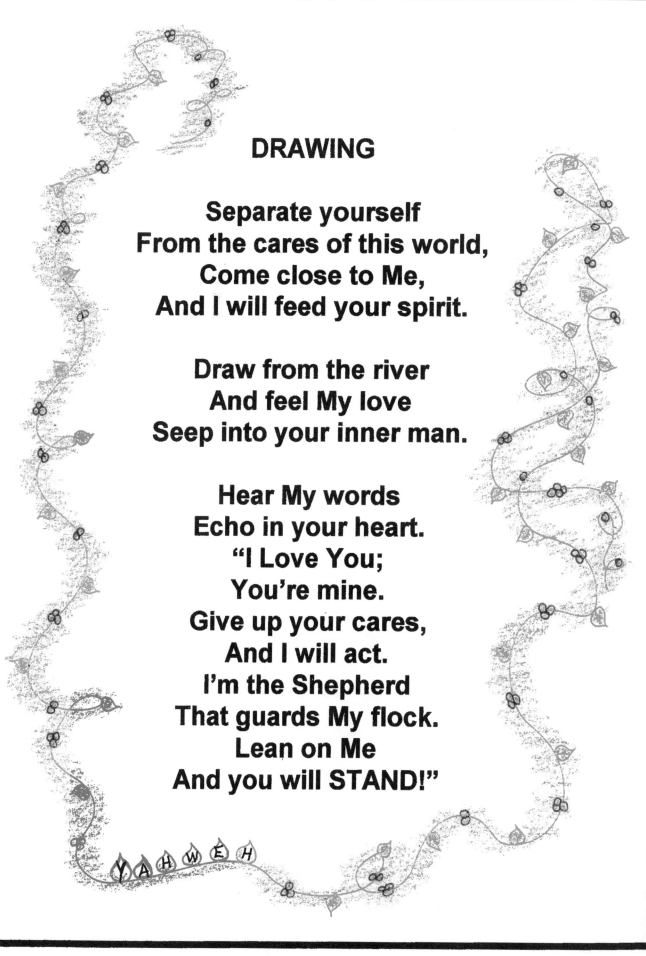

DRAWING

Separate yourself
From the cares of this world,
Come close to Me,
And I will feed your spirit.

Draw from the river
And feel My love
Seep into your inner man.

Hear My words
Echo in your heart.
"I Love You;
You're mine.
Give up your cares,
And I will act.
I'm the Shepherd
That guards My flock.
Lean on Me
And you will STAND!"

YAHWEH

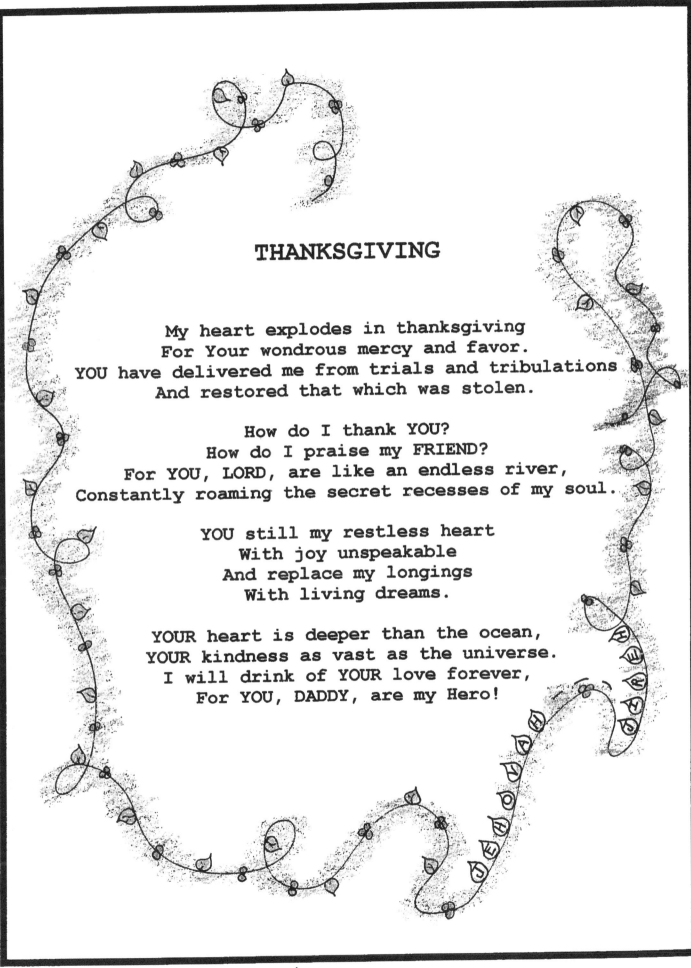

THANKSGIVING

My heart explodes in thanksgiving
For Your wondrous mercy and favor.
YOU have delivered me from trials and tribulations
And restored that which was stolen.

How do I thank YOU?
How do I praise my FRIEND?
For YOU, LORD, are like an endless river,
Constantly roaming the secret recesses of my soul.

YOU still my restless heart
With joy unspeakable
And replace my longings
With living dreams.

YOUR heart is deeper than the ocean,
YOUR kindness as vast as the universe.
I will drink of YOUR love forever,
For YOU, DADDY, are my Hero!

CHINKS

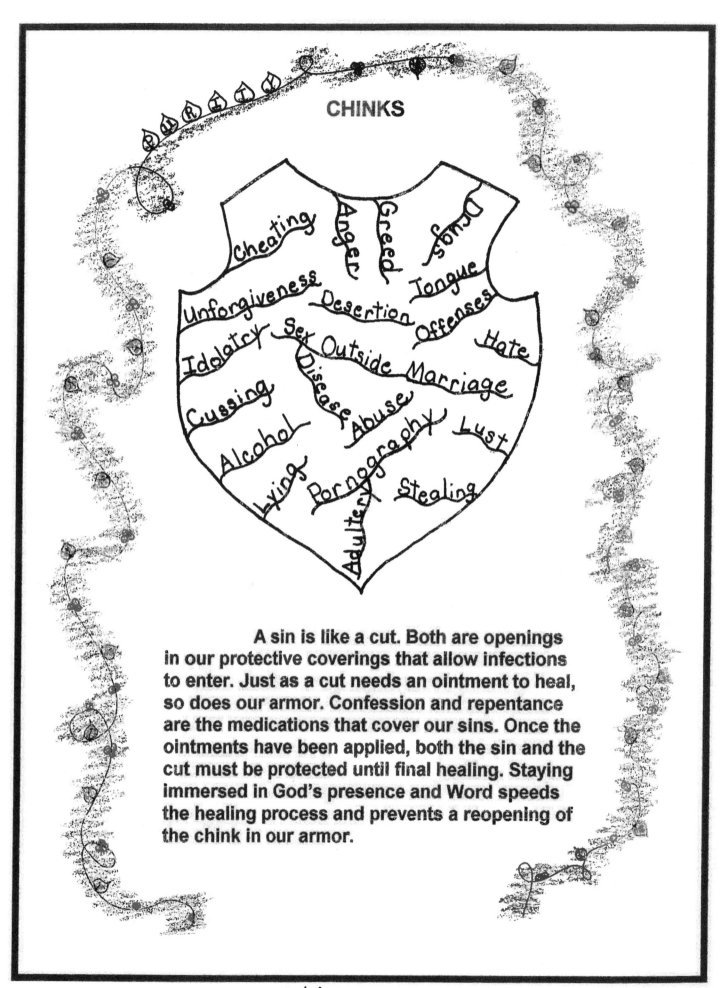

Cheating, Anger, Greed, Drugs, Tongue, Unforgiveness, Desertion, Offenses, Idolatry, Sex Outside Marriage, Hate, Cussing, Disease, Alcohol, Abuse, Lust, Lying, Pornography, Adultery, Stealing

A sin is like a cut. Both are openings in our protective coverings that allow infections to enter. Just as a cut needs an ointment to heal, so does our armor. Confession and repentance are the medications that cover our sins. Once the ointments have been applied, both the sin and the cut must be protected until final healing. Staying immersed in God's presence and Word speeds the healing process and prevents a reopening of the chink in our armor.

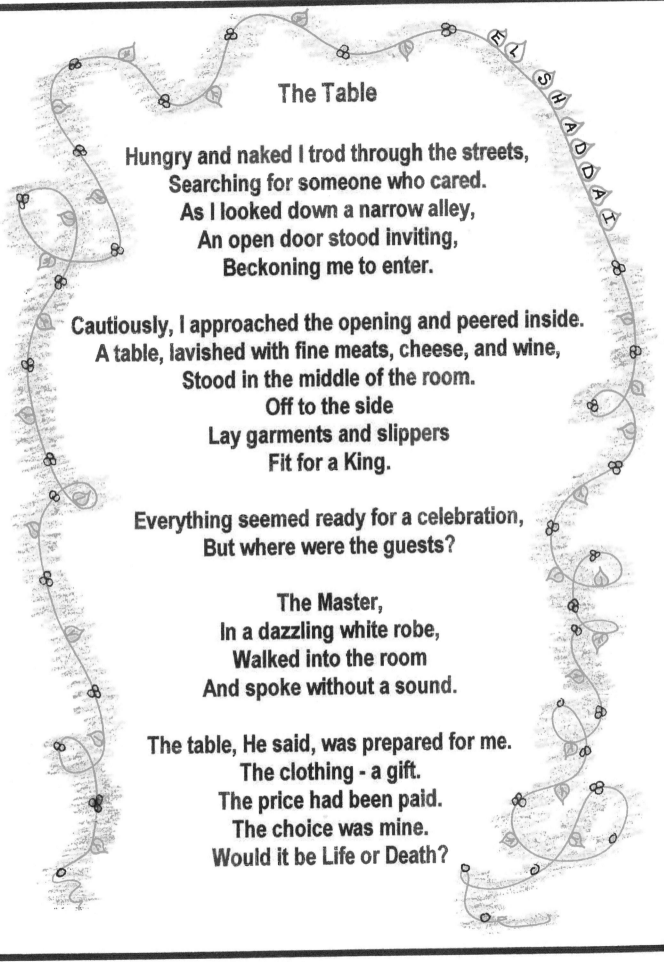

The Table

Hungry and naked I trod through the streets,
Searching for someone who cared.
As I looked down a narrow alley,
An open door stood inviting,
Beckoning me to enter.

Cautiously, I approached the opening and peered inside.
A table, lavished with fine meats, cheese, and wine,
Stood in the middle of the room.
Off to the side
Lay garments and slippers
Fit for a King.

Everything seemed ready for a celebration,
But where were the guests?

The Master,
In a dazzling white robe,
Walked into the room
And spoke without a sound.

The table, He said, was prepared for me.
The clothing - a gift.
The price had been paid.
The choice was mine.
Would it be Life or Death?

62

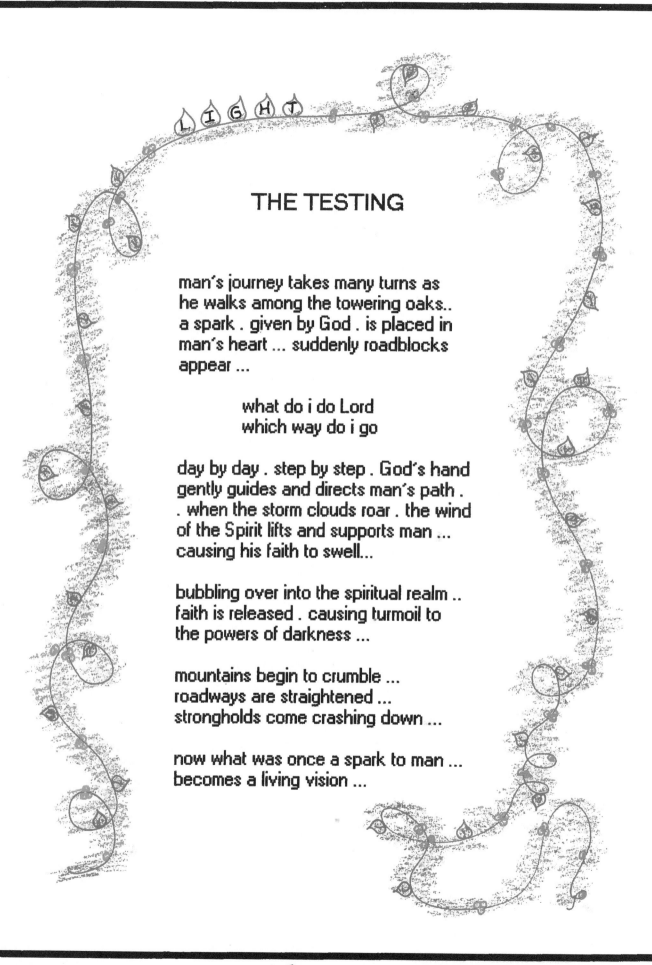

LIGHT

THE TESTING

man's journey takes many turns as
he walks among the towering oaks..
a spark . given by God . is placed in
man's heart ... suddenly roadblocks
appear ...

what do i do Lord
which way do i go

day by day . step by step . God's hand
gently guides and directs man's path .
. when the storm clouds roar . the wind
of the Spirit lifts and supports man ...
causing his faith to swell...

bubbling over into the spiritual realm ..
faith is released . causing turmoil to
the powers of darkness ...

mountains begin to crumble ...
roadways are straightened ...
strongholds come crashing down ...

now what was once a spark to man ...
becomes a living vision ...

STANDING

Man cries daily,
"Why Lord?
Why have You not moved?"

But God replies,
"Son, have you not learned?
Have you not heard?
The Word is the answer.
The Word is the key.

Stand on My covenant.
Stand on My promises.
Speak forth My Word,
And It will come to pass.

For My Word is Life and Light.
It pierces darkness
And brings fears to naught.
Stand, my son, Stand!"

JEHOVAH - ELOHIM

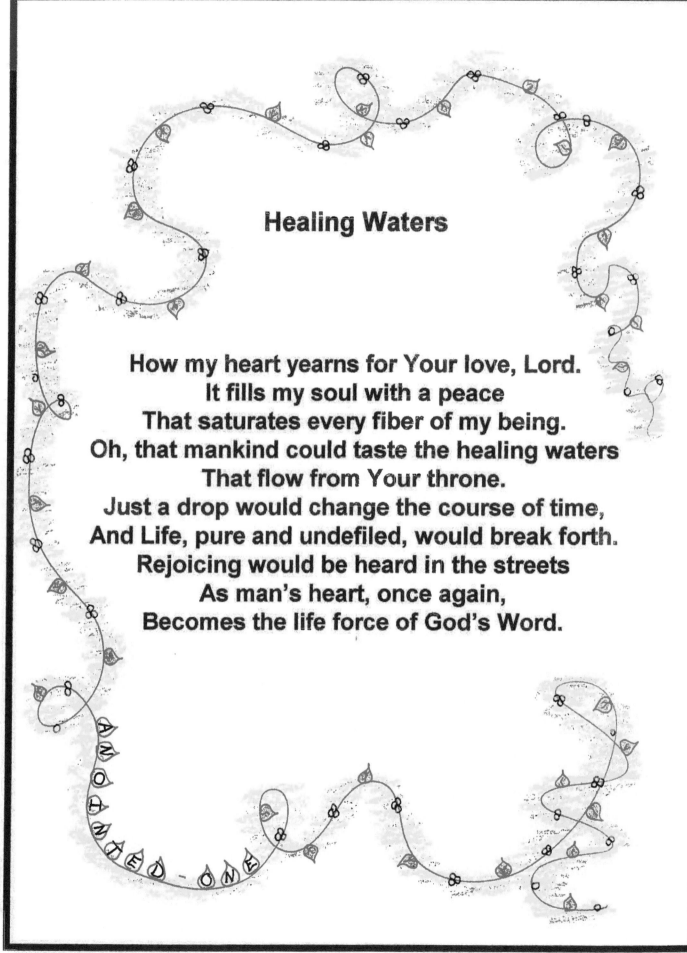

Healing Waters

How my heart yearns for Your love, Lord.
It fills my soul with a peace
That saturates every fiber of my being.
Oh, that mankind could taste the healing waters
That flow from Your throne.
Just a drop would change the course of time,
And Life, pure and undefiled, would break forth.
Rejoicing would be heard in the streets
As man's heart, once again,
Becomes the life force of God's Word.

ANOINTED-ONE

COVERING

As the snow blankets the earth
And covers all imperfections,
So God's love
Covers man's flaws and weaknesses.

Gazing across fields of freshly fallen snow,
Man's eyes behold a scene of redemptive purity.

Speaking through nature,
God teaches His children love.
Through the shed blood of one Son,
Man was redeemed.

The price was paid.
The gift is free.
The choice is man's.
The prize - eternity.

JEHOVAH - NISSH

FAITHFULNESS

Father,
No words can express
How much I love You.
Your faithfulness and love
Are as vast as the universe.

Even though the storm surge roars,
My spirit is at peace.
A confidence swells inside of me,
Dispelling all fears and doubts that arise.

Your love
Covers every part of my being,
Flooding me with a sense of wholeness
I've never known.

No earthly word
Can declare my thanksgiving to You, Daddy,
For Your Presence enfolds my world
And rocks the gates of Hell,
Keeping me safe and unwavering
To become the vision
You've placed in my heart.

67

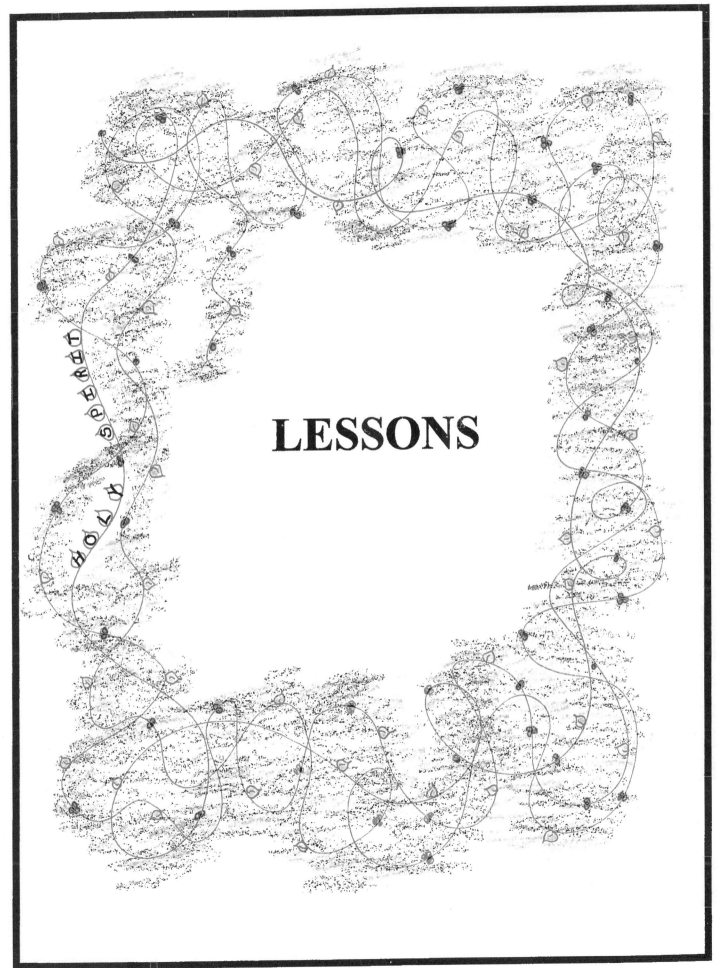

HOLY SPIRIT

LESSONS

Who We Are in Christ

Most Christians never seize the promises God has given them because they fail to understand who they are in Christ. They struggle daily with past mistakes and failures. They don't feel worthy to receive God's blessings because in their eyes they don't deserve His favor. I can say this because there was a time period in my own life that I felt ashamed of all God had given me. As a result, I constantly apologized to anyone who would listen. Thank God I've been redeemed from that bondage.

When I began studying God's Word to find out who I am in Christ, my eyes were opened to the Truth. The New Testament is full of references that refer to *in Him*, *in Christ*, and *in Whom*. We were bought with a price, a high price, that should never be taken lightly. "For God so greatly loved and dearly prized the world that He (even) gave up His only begotten (unique) Son, so that whoever believes in (trusts in, clings to, relies on) Him shall not perish (come to destruction, be lost) but have eternal (everlasting) life." John 3:16 (Amplified Bible)

The first key to understanding is the phrase *in Him*. We must be *in Him* to claim and receive His promises. That does not mean a one time conversion experience, and then God is put on the back burner of our lives. Rather it means a daily, hour by hour, minute by minute, walk with Christ, constantly staying in communion with Him. Every act, thought, and deed should be done to honor and glorify our Lord and Savior.

Now that we understand the importance of *in Him*, *in Whom*, and *in Christ*, let's examine what God's Word says. Ephesians 1:7 states, "*In Him* we have redemption (deliverance and salvation) through His blood, the remission (forgiveness) of our offenses (shortcomings and trespasses), in accordance with the riches and the generosity of His gracious favor." Once we have accepted Christ as our Savior, all our past sins have been forgiven. Our slate is wiped clean, and we have been restored to favor. II Corinthians 5:19 tells us that "if any person is (engrafted) *in Christ* (the Messiah) he is a new creation (a new creation altogether); the old (previous moral and spiritual condition) has passed away. Behold, the fresh and new has come." Thank God for the blood of Jesus. Our past is completely gone, and God has placed a new spirit inside of us. "There is now no condemnation (no judging guilty of wrong) for those who are *in Christ Jesus* (who live and walk not after the dictates of the flesh, but after the dictates of the Spirit.)" Romans 8:1 Now if our past has been erased, then we need to leave it alone - not continually rewrite it. Our salvation is based on faith - faith and trust in Jesus Christ. We must <u>believe</u> to be justified. Are we really trusting in Christ if we allow our past mistakes and past sins to take root in our minds and hearts? God is only glorified and honored when we believe in His Word and act accordingly.

Once the truth that we are a new creation is revealed to us, then we need to press further. What promises and rights do we have *in Christ?* God's Word speaks very clearly about this:

I Cor. 1:4 Grace (unmerited favor) is given us *in Christ Jesus.*

I Cor. 1:5 We are enriched with full power of speech and knowledge *in Christ.*

I Cor. 15:52 We have the promise of being raised from death.

II Cor. 1:20 *In Christ* all God's promises are Yes.

Gal. 3:26 We are sons and daughters of God.

Eph. 1:11 We were made God's heritage and have obtained an inheritance (That should make us shout for joy!)

Eph. 2:6 We have joint seating with Christ in the Heavenly sphere.

Eph. 3:6 We are joint heirs with the Jews, sharing in the same divine promises.

Eph. 6:10 We have strength *in Him.*

Philippians 4:7 God's peace (not man's) shall be ours.

Philippians 4:19 All our needs will be liberally supplied *in Christ.* (We need to lay hold of this and press in by claiming the scripture daily.)

II Tim. 3:17 We are fully equipped for every good work. (Has God called you into a specific service? Then, do not fear or doubt, but trust the One Who said that you are fully equipped for every good labor!)

Each of these scriptures is God's promise to us who believe in His Son, Christ Jesus. However, they are only words on paper until we lay hold of them and claim each one as our own. We are God's sons and daughters who have been given gifts as our inheritance. Galatians 3:29 declares, "And if you belong to Christ (are *in Him* Who is Abraham's Seed), then you are Abraham's offspring and (spiritual) heirs according to promise." Yet, just as in the natural, children can not receive their family's inheritance if they do not go and claim it, so it is in the spiritual. We must vigorously go after and confess each promise the Father has given us. Search the scriptures and find out what God has declared is yours. Lay hold by audibly confessing His Word and believing that what He says will come to pass. (Even though all God's promises are *Yes*, they can not flow into a Christian's life if there is sin in it. Examine yourself, and root out anything that is not of God. II Cor. 13:5 states, "Examine and test and evaluate your own selves to see whether you are holding to your faith and showing the proper fruits of it.")

Just as important as knowing our blood-bought promises *in Christ* is the knowledge that all Christians are joined together to form one body. Romans 12:5 says that "we, numerous as we are, are one body *in Christ* (the Messiah) and individually we are parts one of another (mutually dependent on one another)." Christians have specific parts to play and need to be in the area God has called them - just like the pieces of a puzzle. If just one part (a Christian) is out of place, then the entire body is affected. Ephesians 2:21 declares, "*In Him* the whole structure is joined (bound, welded) together harmoniously, and it continues to rise (grow, increase) into a holy temple in the Lord (a sanctuary dedicated, consecrated, and sacred to the presence of the Lord.)" God needs a unified, holy temple in which to dwell. If someone is not where God has placed him or her, then that believer brings disharmony to the entire body. This is one reason why some churches fail or have no power. The members are out of joint; thus, the structure is weak and frail. God has placed a high calling on His children, and it is important that each one be in his or her position to bring unity and support to the body and its ministry.

BREATH OF LIFE

Love, Holiness, and Fear

"Assemble the people - men, women, and children, and the stranger and the sojourner within your towns - that they may *hear* and *learn* (reverently) to fear the Lord your God and be watchful to do all the words of the law."

Deut. 31:12
(Amplified Bible)

Watching the world change over the last few years, I've often asked the Lord what has happened to His people? Why isn't there a noticeable distinction between those who claim to be Christians and those who are not? Why is sin or the result of sin as prevalent in the Church today as it is in the world? Where is the holiness that God declares must exist in His people? (Lev. 19:1; 1 Peter 1:15)

As I began searching for the answers to these questions, God led me to study three concepts - *love, holiness,* and *fear of the Lord.* Each of these are so intertwined that they become one vine. None can function without the support or strength of the others. We cannot love if we're not holy. We can't be holy if do not revere the Lord. We can't fear God if we do not love.

Reading the scriptures, I began to see the link that brought each vine toward the others and enabled the three to entwine so tightly, that if one part did not function properly, then the whole structure died. In Deut. 4:10, the Lord said, "Gather the people together to Me, and I will make them *hear* My words, that they learn (reverently) to *fear* Me all the days they live upon the earth and that they may teach their children." The key to holiness, love, and reverential fear of the Lord is hearing God's Word. Deut. 31:12 takes this one more step. "That they may *hear* and *learn* (reverently) to fear the Lord your God and be watchful to *do* all the words of the law." We cannot fear the Lord and walk in holiness if our ears and our hearts have not been enlightened. Once we have been enlightened, then we must obey.

Nurturing our ability to love and fear God demands that we first *hear!* That is where most Christians slip and fall. They depend on

72

ministers, TV evangelists, friends, or family to tell them what to do rather then spending their own time in God's presence, reading and studying His Word.

Once I understood the key (God's Word), then I began to search the scriptures to find what God requires of His children. First, what does the Word mean when it says to fear the Lord? To revere God does not mean to shake or tremble, but rather it means to respect, honor, and to obey.

Deut. 5:29 states, "Oh, that they had such a (mind and) heart in them always (reverently) to fear Me and keep all My commandments, that it might go well with them and their children forever."

Genesis 22:12 says that nothing should be held back from God. Abraham was willing to sacrifice his son, Isaac, because he believed God's promises were true.

Deut. 10:12 tells us (the Christian) to serve God with all your heart, mind, and being.

Joshua 24:14 reminds us to fear the Lord in sincerity and truth.

Acts 10:35 states, "But in every nation, he who venerates and has a reverential fear for God, treating Him with worshipful obedience and living uprightly, is acceptable to Him and sure of being received and welcomed (by Him)." Thus, fearing the Lord means to honor God by obeying His Word, by putting Him first in your life, and by serving and praising Him daily.

Next, as I studied the scriptures, I discovered that holiness required obedience the same as the reverential fear of the Lord. 1 Peter 1:15 says, "But as the One Who called you is holy, you yourselves also be holy in all your conduct and manner of living." Thus, we must know what God's Word says about the way we are to live day to day. Again, to *hear* from our Father, we must know His Word.

As I reread the scriptures that had to do with holiness, I found a blueprint of God's plan for our daily walk. Ephesians 4:17 - 5:21 gives the Christian a solid pattern to follow:

Eph. 4:17 Don't live as the world in their perverseness (folly, vanity, etc.).

4:18 Don't lack moral understanding (willful blindness, hardness of heart).

4:19 Don't be callous or have unbridled sensuality, greed, or impurity.

4:22-23 Renew yourself daily.

4:24 Put on God's nature by immersing yourself in His Word and by prayer.

4:25 Always speak truth.

4:26-27 Forgive quickly so that the devil does not find a chink in your armor.

4:28 Do not steal or cheat.

4:29 Guard your words - let no evil or unwholesome talk come out of your mouth.

4:31 Get rid of all bitterness, rage, anger, resentment, slander, temper.

4:32 Be compassionate and forgiving.

5:1-2 Walk in Christ's footsteps.

5:3-5 Immorality, greed, sexual sins, coarse joking, filthiness, or lustful desires for someone else's property should not even be mentioned.

5:7 Don't associate with those who do the above things.

5:10-15 Know what pleases God and be wise.

5:16 Don't get drunk.

5:19-21 Praise and thank the Lord daily.

As God opened my eyes to His truth, I understood how important it is for us to immerse ourselves daily in His Word and do whatever He says to do. God's Word will come to pass as we continually walk in His footsteps and obey.

Just as holiness and the fear of the Lord require obedience to God's Word, so does love. 1 John 5:3 states, "For true love of God is this: that we *do* His commandments (keep His ordinances and are mindful of His precepts and teachings)." Again God says that *obedience* represents *true love.* How can we obey if we do not know? How do we know if we do not hear? The answer is simple. God's Word, His personal letter to every man, woman, and child, opens and enlightens our ears and our hearts to truth. 1 John 4:7 records these words, "Love one another for love springs from God and he who loves his fellowman is begotten (born) of God and is coming (progressively) to know and understand God." The more we know God, the more we understand His character and His heart. John 14:23-24 declares, " If a person really loves Me (Jesus) he will keep My Word (obey My teaching) and My Father will love him, and We will come to him and make Our home (abode, special dwelling place) with him. Anyone who does not (really) love Me does not observe and obey My teachings."

Obedience is not an option, but rather it is a necessity to life. Everyone wants their prayers answered and their dreams to become a reality. Yet, how many Christians pick and choose which teachings to follow and which ones to cast aside. If we truly love our Father, then we follow all of Christ's words.

Lev. 19:18 Love your neighbor as yourself.

Deut. 6:5 Love the Lord your God with all your mind, heart, entire being, and with all your might.

Matt. 5:44 Love your enemies and pray for those who wrong you.

Romans 12:9 Let your love be sincere; hate what is evil.

Romans 12:10 Give precedent and show honor to one another.

1 Cor. 8:1 Love edifies and encourages.

1 Cor. 13:4 Love is patient and kind.

Gal. 5:13 Through love, serve one another.

Phil. 4:8 Think on what is lovely and lovable.

1 Tim. 1:5 Love comes from a pure heart and a clean conscience.

Heb. 1:9 Love righteousness.

1 John 4:18 There is no fear or dread in perfect love.

When we obey, we love; when we love, we honor God. As a result, our lips should constantly swell in praise and adoration. God's divine plan for mankind to walk in victory has been revealed to the world through His Word. Jesus Christ, the living Word, is the door that opens the heart of the Father and allows His Heavenly blessings to overflow in our lives. God's Word becomes our sanctified Bread, filling us daily with food from Heaven. Our spirits, now alive with the Word of God, resound with glorious praise to the One who tore asunder the veil, so that we might enter into the Holy of Holies. All praise, honor, and glory to our Redeemer, our King - The Lord Jesus Christ!

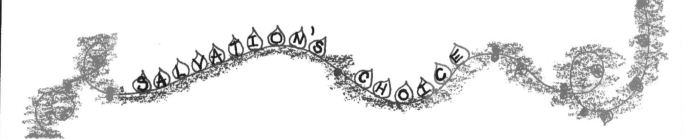

Why Peace?

What is peace? Webster's dictionary says that peace is a state of tranquillity or quiet; a state of security; freedom from oppressive thoughts or emotions; harmony in personal relations. Is this the peace God wants us to have or is God's peace much more than this? John 14:27 states, "Peace I leave with you; My (own) peace I now give and *bequeath* to you. Not as the world gives do I give to you. Do not let your hearts be troubled, neither let them be afraid. (Stop allowing yourselves to be agitated and disturbed; and do not permit yourselves to be fearful and intimidated and cowardly and unsettled.)" How do we attain this peace?

First, we must accept Jesus Christ as our Lord and Savior because Jesus, himself, is our peace. Ephesians 2:14 tells us "that He (Christ) is (Himself) our peace (our bond of unity and harmony)." We must give our hearts and our lives back to God, and then we are free to accept and free to claim this peace. It is a gift *legally* given to those who are in Christ Jesus.

Searching the Word, I began to understand that the peace Christ speaks about is more than just a calm spirit. Yes, if we are truly in Christ Jesus, then we should be free of fear, doubts, worries, and dread. However, there is another area that is linked to peace; and that is prosperity. Isaiah 48:18-19 says, "Oh, that you had hearkened to My commandments! Then your *peace* and *prosperity* would have been like a flowing river, and your righteousness (the holiness and purity of the nation) like the (abundant) waves of the sea. Your offspring would have been like the sand, and your descendants like the offspring of the sea." God is declaring to His people that obedience brings peace and prosperity. In the book of Jeremiah, God tells His prophet that after He has cleansed Judah and Israel of their iniquity, He will restore Jerusalem and "will lay upon it health and healing, and I will cure them and will reveal to them the abundance of peace (*prosperity*, security, stability) and truth." Jeremiah 33:6

There <u>is</u> a connection between peace and prosperity. Some might say, "Well, that was under the covenant in the Old Testament", but God is the same yesterday, today, and forever. If His Word is true and He is no respecter of persons, then what God does for one, He will do for another. As Jesus descended the Mount of Olives, He looked at Jerusalem, wept, and exclaimed, "Would that you had known personally, even at least in this your day, the things that make for peace (for freedom from all the distresses that are experienced as the result of sin and upon which your peace - your security, safety, *prosperity*, and happiness - depends." Luke 19:42

Everyone wants to be prosperous spiritually, physically, financially, socially, and emotionally. Yet, why is it that many of God's children are always in lack? Could one reason be that God's peace is missing in their lives? Christians will always have trials and temptations, but how we react to them determines our state of mind - our peace. Isaiah 26:3 says that "You [God] will guard him [the uncompromising righteous Christian] and keep him in perfect and constant peace whose mind (both its inclination and its character) is stayed in You, because he commits himself to You, leans on You, and hopes confidently in You." To be inclined means to bend or lean or have a natural tendency toward something. Our first reaction to a difficult situation should be to seek our Father's face - to lean on Him completely.

Our emotions or state of mind should not govern or rule our actions or reactions. When we fully understand that peace is linked to our prosperity, as well as our security, then we need to aggressively seek to walk in continual, unfaltering peace. Remember that Jesus said in John 14:27 that He *bequeaths* peace to us. To *bequeath* means to give or leave (personal property) by will. Peace is legally ours because God is bound by His laws and rules. If we obey His statues, then we are entitled to His peace. Every situation, every problem should be brought to God in prayer. The Lord promises in Philippians 4:6-7 that if we bring every circumstance to Him with a thankful heart, that His peace will abide with us always. "And God's peace (shall be yours, that tranquil state of a soul assured of its salvation through Christ, and so fearing nothing from God and being content with its earthly lot of whatever sort that is, that peace) which transcends all understanding shall garrison and mount guard over your hearts and minds in Christ Jesus."

Never forget that walking in peace depends on our relationship and our obedience to God through His Son, Jesus Christ. We can't claim what we do not know, and we can't obey what we do not hear. Only by spending time with a loving Father, can we develop a personal,

MORNING'S SONG

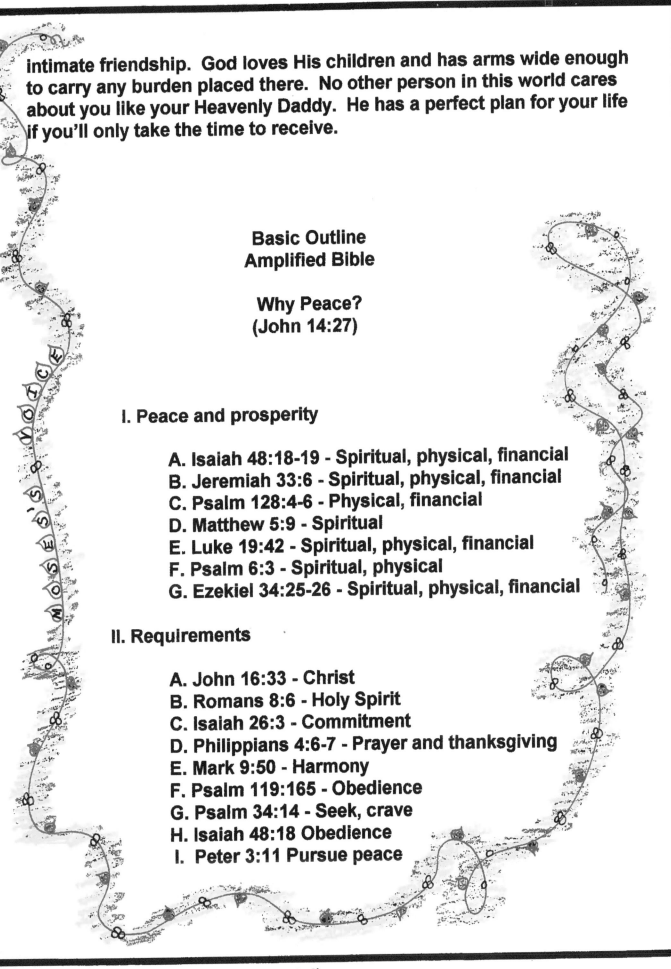

intimate friendship. God loves His children and has arms wide enough to carry any burden placed there. No other person in this world cares about you like your Heavenly Daddy. He has a perfect plan for your life if you'll only take the time to receive.

Basic Outline
Amplified Bible

Why Peace?
(John 14:27)

I. Peace and prosperity

   A. Isaiah 48:18-19 - Spiritual, physical, financial
   B. Jeremiah 33:6 - Spiritual, physical, financial
   C. Psalm 128:4-6 - Physical, financial
   D. Matthew 5:9 - Spiritual
   E. Luke 19:42 - Spiritual, physical, financial
   F. Psalm 6:3 - Spiritual, physical
   G. Ezekiel 34:25-26 - Spiritual, physical, financial

II. Requirements

   A. John 16:33 - Christ
   B. Romans 8:6 - Holy Spirit
   C. Isaiah 26:3 - Commitment
   D. Philippians 4:6-7 - Prayer and thanksgiving
   E. Mark 9:50 - Harmony
   F. Psalm 119:165 - Obedience
   G. Psalm 34:14 - Seek, crave
   H. Isaiah 48:18 Obedience
   I. Peter 3:11 Pursue peace

My Heavenly Account

You must tithe if you want a heavenly account. Is tithing for today, or was it only for the ones under the old covenant?

1. Malachi 3:10-11 God says to bring the whole tithe [the entire tenth] into the storehouse.

2. Deut. 26: 1-3 "When you come into the land which the Lord your God gives you as an inheritance and possess it and live in it. You shall take the first of all the produce of the soil which you harvest from the land the Lord your God gives you and put it in a basket, and go to the place [sanctuary] which the Lord your God has chosen as the abiding place for His name. [**This would be your church.**] And you shall go to the priest [**minister**] who is in office in those days and say to him, I give thanks this day to the Lord your God that I have come to a land which the Lord swore to our fathers to give us."

3. Hebrews 7:8 "Here [in the Levitical priesthood] tithes are received by the men who are subject to death; while there [in the case of Melchizedek], they are received by one [**Jesus**] of whom it is testified that he lives [perpetually]."

Hebrews 3:1 Jesus is the consecrated and set apart one. He is our High Priest. Tithing is for today! If Jesus lives perpetually, then we continue to give Him our tithe [a tenth]. **[Now - How do we set up our Heavenly ACCOUNT?]**

4. Philippians 4:15-17 " You Philippians well know that in the early days of the Gospel ministry, when I left Macedonia, no church [assembly] entered into partnership with me and opened up [a debt and credit] ACCOUNT in giving and receiving except you. Not that I seek or am eager for [your] gift, but I do seek and am eager for the harvest of blessings that is accumulating in your ACCOUNT. And my God will supply [fill to the full] your every need according to His riches in glory in Christ Jesus." **[This also goes with Malachi 3:10-11]**

5. I Timothy 6:17-19 " As for the rich in this world, charge them not to be proud and arrogant and contemptuous of others, nor to set their hopes on uncertain riches, but on God, who richly and ceaselessly provides us with everything for our enjoyment. [Charge them] to do good, to be rich in good work, to be liberal and generous of heart, ready to share [with others]. In this

way laying up for themselves [the riches that endure forever as] a good foundation for the future, so that they may grasp that which is life indeed."

6. Ephesians 6:8 " Knowing that for whatever good anyone does, he will receive his reward from the Lord, whether he is slave or free."

7. Mark 4:7-8 " Other seed [of the same kind] fell among thorn plants, and the thistles grew and pressed together and utterly choked and suffocated it, and it yielded no grain. And other seed [of the same kind] fell into good [well-adapted] soil and brought forth grain, growing up and increasing and yielding up to thirty times as much, and sixty times as much, and even a hundred times as much as had been sown." **You take the seed {the WORD] and obey it. Each time you do what the WORD says, you are planting a seed [Which is the WORD] and will receive a harvest. You must speak forth God's promises and claim them**.

8. Mark 4:29 " But when the grain is ripe and permits, immediately he sends forth [the reapers] and puts in the sickle because the harvest stands ready." **Malachi 3:11 reinforces this concept. God rebukes the devourer [devil] , and he cannot destroy your fruit before it is ready to be harvested. God has His children put deposits into their ACCOUNT before they need them. By reading and obeying God's Word, by tithing and giving offerings, and by giving of your time and talents unselfishly, your ACCOUNT will be full and ready to be withdrawn.**

When a need arises, you find and claim the scripture[s] which states that God will supply your need [whatever it may be], and lay hold of it. Remind God of your heavenly account and stand, knowing that God will supply your every need.

STRENGTH AND SHIELD

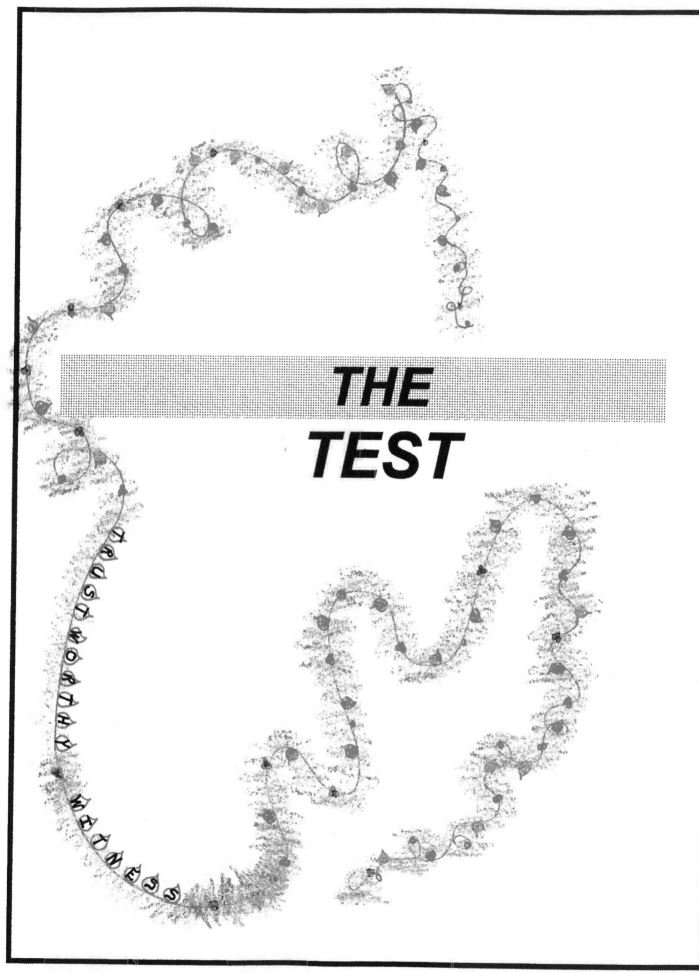

THE
TEST

TRUSTWORTHY WITNESS

On Tuesday, September 26, 2000, the life of my family was changed dramatically forever. My 26 year-old son, Robert, was involved in a head-on collision on his way to work. Even though that morning dawned like any other morning, a life-changing, life-altering event began to unwind. God in His infinite wisdom had been preparing us for months for what was about to happen. My son and his wife, Christina, had just emerged from their own personal faith experience, believing and sowing seeds that were soon to be harvested. God had been "directing and establishing our steps" (Psalm 37:23) over the last two to three years. He had taught us about His Word, His Covenant, His Truth, and His Faithfulness. Everything was ready; seeds had been planted; and support was in place. Thus began the greatest journey of faith my family had ever walked.

Early Tuesday, around 8:00AM, Rob was hit by another car. The driver, going off the side of the road, lost control of her car and plowed into my son's car, pushing him into the hillside. Unconscious and bleeding internally, Rob appeared lifeless. Satan seemed to have won, but God was there, bringing everything and everyone into place. Within minutes, help arrived. A minister, who was traveling in the area, stopped at the accident. Realizing that Rob was still alive, he said a short prayer for the Lord Jesus to save him. (A Word spoken forth that brought Life.) Soon emergency teams converged at the site. Because of the condition of the car, the jaws-of-life had to be used to extricate him. No one understood why Rob was still alive. (He had a torn aorta, ruptured spleen, broken and crushed bones around the left eye, broken right ankle, head injury, internal bleeding, and a tear in his liver.) He needed to be flown to Ruby Memorial Hospital at West Virginia University, but the weather conditions made it impossible for Health Net to land. First critical decision - which hospital? Even though the paramedics believed Rob would die, they decided to take him to W.Va. University (over an hour away) instead of the closest hospital. [Divine Wisdom]

FAITHFUL ONE

Upon arrival, doctors began to evaluate Rob's condition. Then papers were signed, and emergency surgery began. Teams of doctors performed procedures to remove his spleen and repair his aorta. During this time period, a close family friend brought two healing scripture books to us from a Kenneth Hagin conference. These books, Healing for the Whole Man and Healing Scriptures, along with the Bible became our life force over the next several days and weeks. (God had already prepared the way for Rob's complete recovery.)

When the doctors told us that afternoon that Rob was having complications in surgery, we gathered, as a group of believers who knew the power of God's Word, and began to speak forth healing scriptures. We prayed in the chapel, in hallways, in waiting rooms, and anywhere God led us. Seeds of faith were planted in our spirits as we spoke His Word in each situation. When the surgeries were completed around 5 PM that first day, doctors informed us that they had done all they could, but Rob's lungs were filled with fluid; (They had given him 50 units of fluid) his blood wasn't clotting; and his oxygen level was around 30-40%. However, when you sow seeds of faith and the Word, God's supernatural gifts appear. The gift of faith began to swell up inside of us as we continued praying and speaking scriptures. God SPOKE the world into existence, and we were speaking forth His healing Word.

Around 9:30 PM that night, the chief of staff met with the family and informed us Rob would probably not make it till morning. Because he was not getting enough oxygen, his heart would fail. We stood and said that Rob *would live* and that God *would provide* whatever Rob needed (Gift of Faith). We continued to pray specifically for Rob's body, using scriptures from Healing for the Whole Man and Healing Scriptures. We covered every organ, every situation, every nurse, every doctor with the blood and the Word. We expected God to move because we and Rob were in covenant with El Elyon (God Most High), and He does not lie!

That night and the days and nights that followed were used by a loving Father to teach and show His children that His Word is Power and Truth, that the Lord's blood covers everything and opens the way to eternal life and blessings. He taught us to guard our ears and our thoughts - that "when the enemy comes in like a flood, the Spirit of the Lord will lift up a standard against him" (Isaiah 59:19). We were in a battle, and the Lord was teaching us to stand, stand, stand!

That first week the Holy Spirit gave us a Rhema Word for Rob's healing - Isaiah 58:8. "Then shall your light break forth like the morning and your health shall spring forth speedily." We placed this scripture on the side of Rob's bed, so it would be a constant reminder of God's promise to us. We pinned a prayer cloth that had been anointed and prayed over on his neck brace. We prayed the Blood of Christ over everything that touched Rob's body and over every word that was spoken in his room.

As Rob's physical condition began to stabilize, a new concern developed. Because he had gotten only 30-40% of oxygen for several hours, doctors believed that Rob would have brain damage and probably not awaken. Again, we refused the doctors words and spoke forth scriptures for a sound mind. This time, we claimed another Rhema Word - Isaiah 60:1. "Arise, shine, for your light has come, and the glory of the Lord has risen upon you." God confirmed this scripture several times over the next few days. Ben, a Christian nurse, stated that as he administered care that first week, he felt the glory of God all over Rob's body. Also, a close friend of Christina brought a tape that spoke on the Glory and its manifestation. The Lord's healing power was evident in all aspects of Rob's recovery.

During the next several weeks, God continued to confirm to us what we knew would come to pass through His Word. A relative of a family member had been praying for Rob when God gave her a vision. She saw six angels, one each at Rob's head and feet and two on each side with their hands placed strategically on his body, releasing God's healing. Later, a minister's wife called to tell us about a vision two people had during a prayer service for Rob. Each had seen angels surrounding him. Neither person knew anything about the other's vision.

As time passed, Rob continued to improve slowly. However, with every improvement came a new concern. The forces of evil were not going to give up easily, and we had to battle daily for each victory. God was teaching us how to fight and how to stand on His promises. Many times in our natural eyes, the situation looked bleak, but we kept our eyes focused on God's Word and His promises, always speaking forth Life. It's vital when someone is going through a trial to keep close to the Lord, to guard his or her ears from negative (death) comments, and to know the Lord's heart through prayer. God gave us specific directions during those days and weeks; and if we had not spent the time seeking the Lord's face daily, we might have missed that still small voice.

The Bible states in Proverbs 28:18, "Where there is no vision [no redemptive revelation of God] the people perish." Because of this scripture, I asked God for a vision to place before my eyes to guard my faith. He gave me two that I would use over and over the next several months as a shield against the enemy's arsenal of weapons. The first vision was of Rob's mind. I saw the brain divided into two parts; the left side was lit with hundreds of tiny lights, but the right side was in darkness. Then, one by one, lights began to appear until the entire right side of the brain was engulfed with brilliant light. Nerve impulses traveled back and forth sending messages throughout Rob's nervous system. The Lord, I believe, gave Rob new brain cells, for "nothing is impossible for God." (Luke 1:7)

The second vision I received was to keep me focused on the end fulfillment of God's word - complete and total healing of Rob's physical body. I saw him playing football with Colin, who was one year old at the time of the accident, with another small boy hanging onto Rob's leg and a daughter watching from the sidelines. These visions, which were always before my eyes, enabled me to battle every negative thought, word, or comment.

Throughout this trial, God poured blessings into our lives by giving us the privilege of being used by Him to help others in need. Because of our faith walk, we became vessels the Father could use to pour life and His Word into many people. The Holy Spirit opened doors, prepared hearts, and made paths straight for the love of Christ to be poured out, bringing healing and restoration to hurting souls. Truly, what the enemy had meant for destruction, God was turning into a blessing for our family.

Because of God's faithfulness, my family will never be the same. He has taught us about trust, obedience, and truth. His praises will always be on our lips. Right in the middle of the battle, God told us to praise Him, and that is exactly what we did! We asked our pastors to have a special praise song sung during Sunday morning service. Throughout our area, churches gave God praise for who He is and what He was doing. As the tribe of Judah (Judah means praise) led the Israelites into battle, so our praises opened the door for God's Glory to be revealed. LIVING STONE.

There is no magic formula for victory in this world, only by one name – the name of Jesus. If you belong to the Father, it's only by the shed blood of His Son. Jesus opened the door so that we might enter the promise land. And "all God's promises are yes in Christ." (II Cor. 1:20).

I've tried to share my family's remarkable journey of faith. Even as I write, Rob is still standing fast on God's assurance that he will be completely restored to health, that there will be "nothing missing, nothing broken" (peace shalom) in his life. Rob is now walking with only a slight limp and is getting physically stronger every day. The greatest miracles we have experienced were not the ones during those first few days after the accident, but they have been the small steps of grace that have enabled Rob to trust God for each step forward and for each victory. Healing, our Father has shown us, is by faith, by the Word, and by love.

*Rob is working now and has just written a short book, <u>Unthinkable</u>, about his accident and recovery.

God's
Voice for Today

THE KING

"For this is he that was spoken of by the prophet Isaiah, saying, The voice of one crying in the wilderness, Prepare the Way of the Lord, Make His paths straight."

Matthew 3:3

Over the past few years, the Lord's voice has changed. I have felt an intense urgency in my spirit. No one knows the hour or day the Lord will return; but we are to be ready all the time, for the Son of Man will come when least expected. (Luke 12:40) These prophetic poems have been given to me to share not only with the body of Christ but also with the lost, those searching for God's Light.

Through the anointing of the Holy Spirit, my focus, my thoughts, and my direction have changed. God's voice is more insistent, more pressing, more targeted than ever before. His calling compels each of us to constrain, to bind the power of the enemy so that the lost and hurting will discover their Savior. My prayer for each one who journeys with me through these last pages is to understand the truth of the Lord's Heart! Allow the Spirit's Words to guide and to direct your actions and decisions. Become that arrow that the Lord sends forth to accomplish His purpose and plan on earth.

BREAD OF LIFE

Pure PEACE

Peace, Peace, God's Holy Peace

Fill my soul and mind

Wrap me in Your atoning love

Quenching all worry and doubt

Draw me, Holy Spirit

Into the deepest part of God

Where freedom reigns, and love flows

Changing hearts and minds

Soaring above the chaos below

Cocooned in the Savior's arms

Knowing that God's will shall prevail

Victorious in every battle fought

Adonai protects His Own

His Holy Angels standing guard

Swords drawn, shields in place

A mighty force to behold

Wait, wait, the battle is won

Not by force or by strength

But by the Sword of the Spirit

The Spoken Word of God!

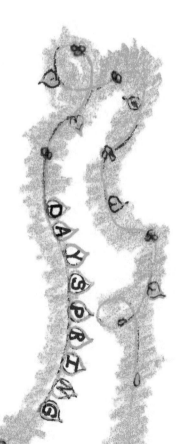

89.

God's Glorious Rain

Rain, rain, God's glorious rain

Falling down, falling down

Consuming His children

Saturating each one with His anointing

Step in, step in while the water cascades

Filling each vessel till it overflows

Droplets, droplets everywhere

Announcing the King's power and authority

Little waterfalls roaming the earth

Depositing God's love and His Glory

Touch, taste, smell His Presence

As He lifts each burden that's carried

See, see, don't you see

A new wave of revival has come

Opening the hearts of each man, woman, child

For the soon returning SON!

90.

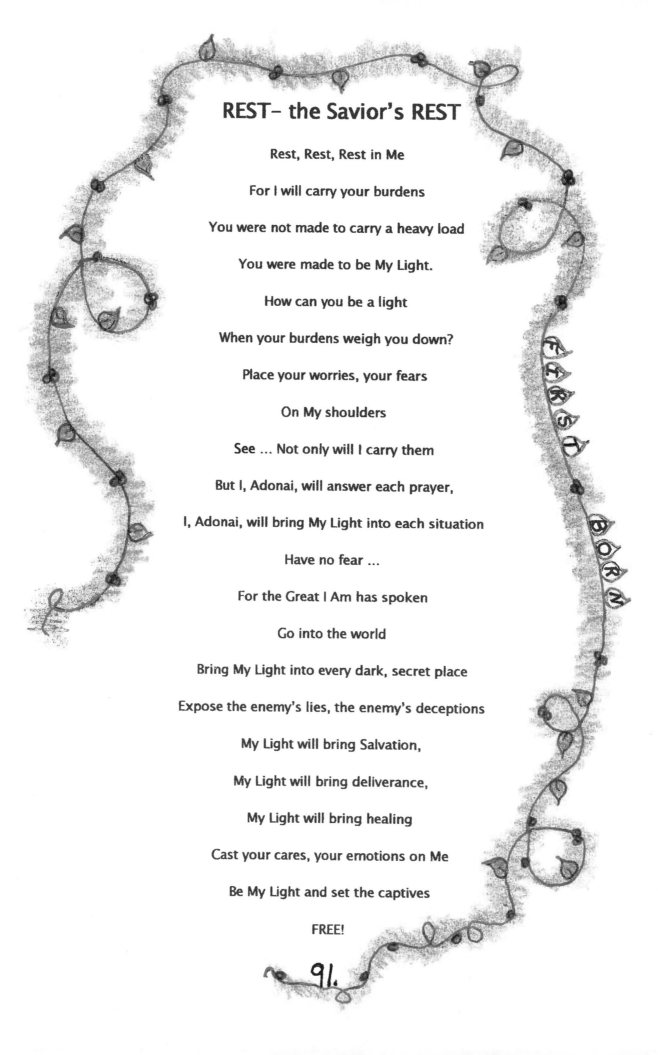

REST– the Savior's REST

Rest, Rest, Rest in Me

For I will carry your burdens

You were not made to carry a heavy load

You were made to be My Light.

How can you be a light

When your burdens weigh you down?

Place your worries, your fears

On My shoulders

See ... Not only will I carry them

But I, Adonai, will answer each prayer,

I, Adonai, will bring My Light into each situation

Have no fear ...

For the Great I Am has spoken

Go into the world

Bring My Light into every dark, secret place

Expose the enemy's lies, the enemy's deceptions

My Light will bring Salvation,

My Light will bring deliverance,

My Light will bring healing

Cast your cares, your emotions on Me

Be My Light and set the captives

FREE!

91.

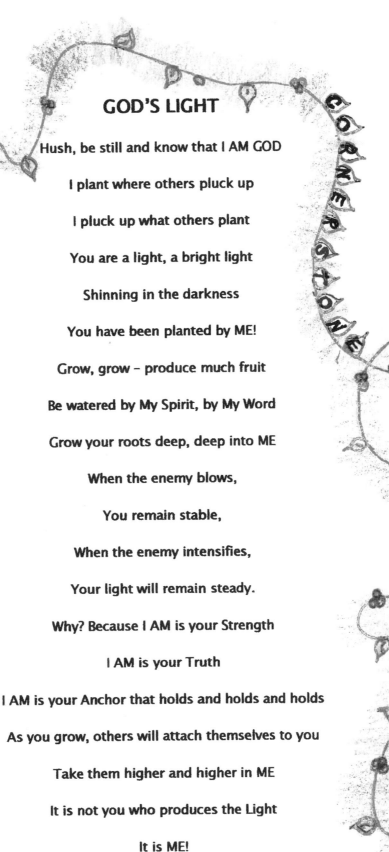

GOD'S LIGHT

Hush, be still and know that I AM GOD

I plant where others pluck up

I pluck up what others plant

You are a light, a bright light

Shinning in the darkness

You have been planted by ME!

Grow, grow – produce much fruit

Be watered by My Spirit, by My Word

Grow your roots deep, deep into ME

When the enemy blows,

You remain stable,

When the enemy intensifies,

Your light will remain steady.

Why? Because I AM is your Strength

I AM is your Truth

I AM is your Anchor that holds and holds and holds

As you grow, others will attach themselves to you

Take them higher and higher in ME

It is not you who produces the Light

It is ME!

Stay anchored and watch . . .

The Great I AM manifest His Glory!

92.

God So LOVED...

That's My Word to you, My little ones

My love covers ALL

Walk in My love

See through My love

Know that nothing happens that I don't already know

That I have a plan for deliverance

Only seek Me

Listen as I speak

Obey My Word

Walk in My Word

Love in My Word

For love covers a multitude of sins

Love opens doors that I have placed before you

Walk in that pure love

My Will, My Plan shall manifest

When My children love.

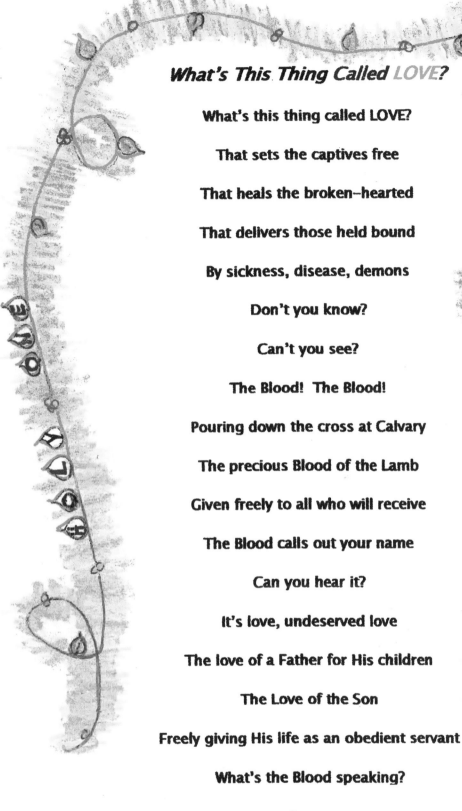

What's This Thing Called LOVE?

What's this thing called LOVE?

That sets the captives free

That heals the broken–hearted

That delivers those held bound

By sickness, disease, demons

Don't you know?

Can't you see?

The Blood! The Blood!

Pouring down the cross at Calvary

The precious Blood of the Lamb

Given freely to all who will receive

The Blood calls out your name

Can you hear it?

It's love, undeserved love

The love of a Father for His children

The Love of the Son

Freely giving His life as an obedient servant

What's the Blood speaking?

Jesus

Jesus

Jesus

The Blood

Be silent no longer

Let the weak say, "I am strong!"

Let the sick say, "I am healed!"

For the Glory of the LORD

Is performing a mighty work

Among HIS people

No longer will the enemy say,

      "Aha, I bring destruction

      I bring pain, sickness, disease"

For the Glory of the LORD shines brightly

HIS anointing crushes the head of the enemy

Don't you see?

Don't you perceive?

Blind eyes are opened

Deaf ears hear again

Shout from the roof tops ...

My GOD reigns!

My GOD is victorious!

The enemy has been defeated

By the Blood of the Lamb!

Walk in wholeness

For HIS blood covers HIS people!

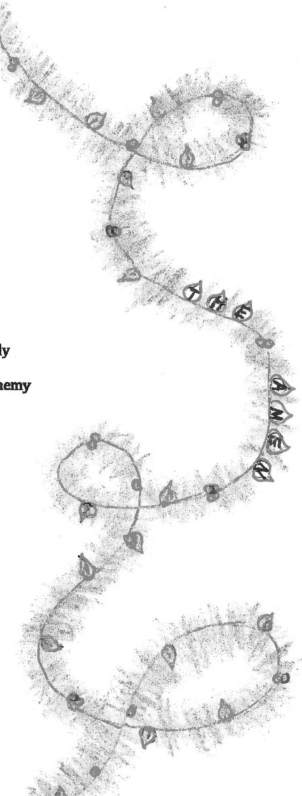

95.

A Call to Battle

The Lion of the Tribe of Judah says, Come!

Rise up oh mighty army of God.

The battle is ready? The fields are ripe.

Soar with the eagles.

Complete the work you have been called to do.

Are you ready? Do you know?

Do you perceive what's ahead?

Put on the full, complete armor of God.

The enemy cannot touch God's anointed!

Why fear? Why worry?

Greater is He who is within you than he who is in the world!

My people are dying.

Snatch them out of the enemy's hand.

Stand Strong!

Know who you are, my sons and daughters.

The Great I Am is your Father.

He lives in you. Stand Strong!

Battle lines have been drawn.

Will you stand and fight?

Stand Strong! Don't give up!

The victory has already been won!

STAND STRONG!

96.

GOD's ARROW

Marching, marching,

Forward, forward,

Don't stop, don't look back,

Keep your eyes on the prize

Reach toward Heaven's calling

Upward, upward,

Your arrow is your guide

Its path is straight and narrow

It's designed especially for you, my child,

It will never miss its mark

For My Hands will guide it.

Shoot My arrow

Watch it fly

Did you see it?

Bull's eye!

It will accomplish My purpose

Wait on ME – then . . .

Aim . . .

Shoot . . .

My arrow wins each battle

For it's designed by the CREATOR

To be VICTORIOUS!

Come Up

As the Heavens open

The rain comes down

A Voice calls out

"Come up, come up higher."

Suddenly a hand pulls me upward

The rain saturating my soul

Filling me with heavenly gifts

Till I'm overflowing with God's Spirit.

"My son, you are ready now

Go forth in the anointing and power

That emanates from My Shkhinah

Know that I've equipped you

To release upon this Earth

My divine plan.

Heal the sick

Break the chains that bind

Set the captives free.

As My Word is released

Dunamis power explodes

Demonic and foe bow down

All submit to My Will

Watch and stand still

Hear the sound of victory

The spotless blood of the Lamb triumphs

Rejoice all ye people of God.

98.

The Call

The Lord reigns and rules over all the earth

His righteousness endures forever

He rests His hand upon those who fear Him

Anointing His servants with power from on high

His children go forth proclaiming the wonders of the Almighty

Raising the dead, healing the sick

Casting out each demon that interferes with the Master's plan

Nothing, no nothing can stand when the Greatest on High speaks

For He seeks those who are hungry

Those who are searching

Those who harken to His call

Are you ready? Have you heard?

That still small voice speaks

Listen...Listen... the Master calls

Step out; step in as the anointing flows

Cloth yourself with the Spirit

Go, do as He commands

Spread the Word, share the gifts

For the time is short

The Lord wants none to parish

Go... Do... as He commands!

BATTLE CRY

A shaking, a shaking is coming

The battle lines have been drawn.

Who is on the LORD's side?

Who stands for truth?

Not in word, but in deed

All hindrances cast aside

Eyes straight ahead

Marching, marching forward

Count the cost

Victory is not easy

But available to those

Who stand, who pray

Who stand, who pray

Who stand, who pray

Watching, listening for the Call

Hear the trumpet?

Now is the time

There is no turning back

The Heavens are opening

The LIGHT shines forth

The BATTLE has begun.

100.

Time to Seek

If you seek Me, you will find Me,

If you call upon Me, I will answer.

For those who seek, desire My wisdom,

For those who call, know My voice.

My children, My children,

To grow closer to Me requires sacrifice,

Your time, your devotion, your love,

Your obedience, your very self.

Daily I wait for you

Did you call today?

Did you seek My face?

Distractions, roadblocks, stumbling stones,

The enemy demands your time, your soul!

I have anointed you to do great and mighty deeds

Where are your priorities?

Only one thing I desire – you!

Seek Me first in all your ways

And everything else will be added unto you!

Hear ye, people of God

Great is your God!

If I be lifted up,

I will draw all men to Me!

LIFT ME UP!

Seek and you shall find.

Knock and doors will be opened.

Enter through the narrow gate

Don't turn to the right or left.

Keep your eyes, your heart, fixed on Me.

Let Me guide and direct you

Listen, Listen to My Voice.

The days are growing dark

Let your light shine in the darkness

Be My Hands and Feet

Be My Voice to a lost and dying world.

Be Prepared!

Be Ready!

Soon, very soon, you will see Me

When you stand before Me, what will you hear?

Well done thy good and faithful servant!   OR

Depart from Me, I never knew you!

The choice is yours

Choose the narrow road

For great will be your reward!

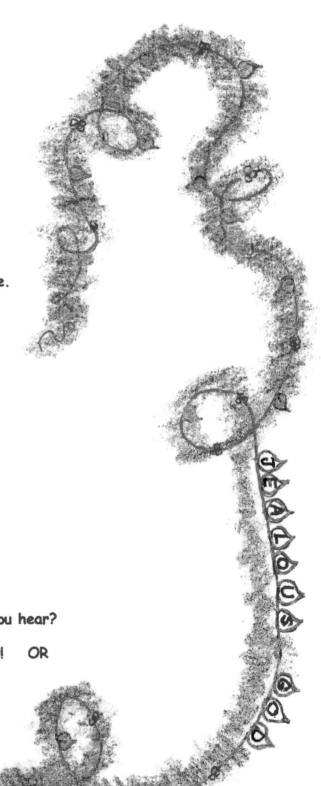

102.

A CALL TO WAR

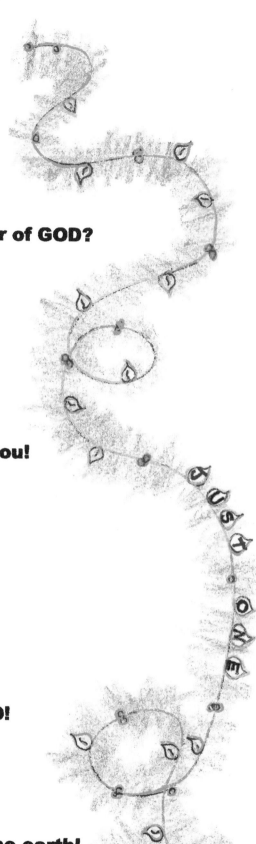

A call to war has sounded

Soldiers are you ready?

Are you equipped with the full armor of GOD?

The battle has begun

Take your positions and wait!

Wait till the call goes out

Don't fear! Don't tremble!

The LORD your GOD will fight with you!

HE will be your Shield!

HE will move upon you

To bring deliverance, healing

To set the captives free!

March, march forward!

Be amazed at the power of your GOD!

Eye has not seen

Ear has not heard

The SOUNDS of Victory that circle the earth!

The Sign of the Times

Restlessness welling up inside

Searching, looking for what's ahead.

A door has closed, but look ....

Another one has opened

Do I dare enter?

"What's just beyond the door, Lord?"

The Spirit says, "Come,

For great and mighty wonders lie ahead.

Be bold, be brave, be strong

Enter while there is time

Are you prepared for what's about to happen?"

A fire burns deep within me

Urging me forward.

As I step inside the door

A consuming presence floods my soul

Filling me, preparing me for signs and wonders

There is no more - *I, me, self*

Just a stream of liquid LOVE flowing forth

Healing, delivering, freeing all bound by chains

Are you ready to step inside?

The Spirit softly calls,

COME

COME

ENTER

LIVING STONE

104.

AWAKE

Awake, Arise, the Spirit calls

The summons has gone forward

Be Prepared!

Put on the full armor of God

With your feet firmly planted on the WORD!

Soldiers ready for war

Orders are being sent forth

To take back the dying, the broken, the bruised

Can you hear the roar of the LION

Calling each warrior out

The way has been prepared

March, March, March forward

God's army is arrayed in splendor

For His Glory surrounds each soldier

Causing fear in demonic beings

They tremble, falling to the ground

As the WORD slices back and forth, back and forth

Destroying every scheme, every plan of destruction

Look! Power and authority are encased in God's WORD

Angels shout from the Heavens,

"The enemy has fallen, the enemy has fallen

God's WORD is truth; Righteousness is restored

Victory has been won by the BLOOD

The LION of the Tribe of Judah stands

As KING of KINGS and LORD of LORDS!"

Are You Ready?

What will people say, what will people say

When time is up

Running to and fro

Right and left, left and right

Searching and looking for what?

The trumpet has sounded

All that remains is judgement.

Did you wait too long?

Didn't you hear the Master calling,

Tugging, pulling on your heart.

"Why, why didn't we respond?

We felt His loving touch,

We heard that still small voice,

Calling us home.

Lord, is it too late?

Can we still come home?

We'll be good; we'll work hard."

But the door has closed

Time has run out!

Can you hear the noise?

Wailing, weeping, and gnashing of teeth.

A soft whisper calls,

"The door is almost closed.

Hurry, hurry — come home My child."

The Master reaches forth His hand ...

Will you take it?

106.

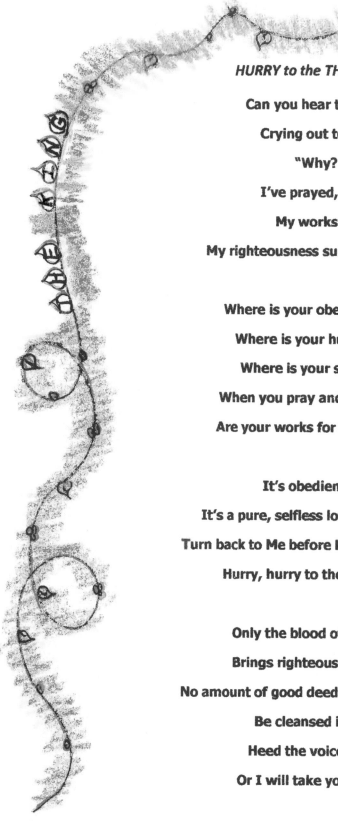

HURRY to the THRONE of GRACE

Can you hear them pleading,

Crying out to the Father

"Why? Why?

I've prayed, I've fasted,

My works increase,

My righteousness surpasses all the rest."

Where is your obedience, My child?

Where is your humble attitude?

Where is your sacrificial love?

When you pray and fast, is it for Me?

Are your works for your own benefit?

It's obedience I desire

It's a pure, selfless love that opens doors.

Turn back to Me before Heaven's gate is closed.

Hurry, hurry to the throne of Grace

Only the blood of My Son, Jesus

Brings righteousness and peace

No amount of good deeds can bring redemption

Be cleansed in the blood

Heed the voice of the Lord

Or I will take your light away.

Hear me, child ... For I will come quickly and the door will shut

Don't delay, come back home

TIME IS SHORT   TIME IS SHORT

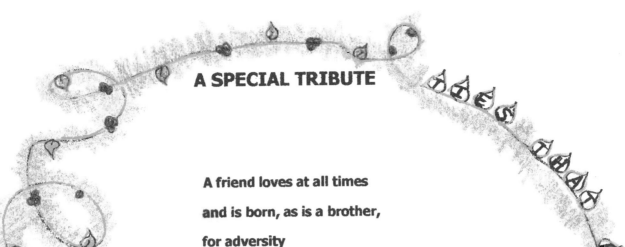

A SPECIAL TRIBUTE

A friend loves at all times

and is born, as is a brother,

for adversity

Proverbs 17:17

This book has been an outpouring of GOD's love and direction in my life. My prayer to all who walked with me through this book is that your journey may be lighter, knowing that the MASTER never deserted me but sustained me through difficult times and lifted my head when the weariness of the battle seemed to shut out all light.

Some of the blessings of a loving FATHER are the roots HE places in your life to strengthen you and hold you fast when the winds and raging fire intensify. These roots not only uphold you but bear the burdens when the heaviness shatters your spirit. They bring peace and order back into your world.

My deepest love and appreciation are given to the roots that ABBA placed in my life. You are the friends whom I cherish and respect for standing with me over the years and bringing healing to my soul. This book is a reflection of your faithfulness and obedience to our FATHER.

I love you!

Jennifer

Sharon

Connie Ann

Kandi

What a privilege,
What an honor,
To be called
Child of the Great
I AM

CPSIA information can be obtained
at www.ICGtesting.com
Printed in the USA
FSHW011855070219
55501FS

9 781545 624241